The Junior Swordsman

A Daily Bible Reading Guide for Kids
Volume 1
The Gospels

By Evangelist Bill Robelen

Robelen Revival Publishing

Copyright © 2020 Bill Robelen
All rights reserved. No portion of this book may be reproduced in any form without written permission from the publisher, except for brief excerpts for reviews and commentary.

Unless otherwise indicated, all scripture quotations are from the King James Version.

ISBN 978-0-578-69803-8

Aknowledgements

I would like to thank my wife, Pollyanna for all of her advice and encouragement. I would also like to thank my editor, Susan Hartwell for her patient work showing all my flaws.

Foreword

Why write this book? In my work with children's ministries, I have often heard people tell children that they need to read the Bible to grow as Christians, but they never provided a plan for them to do so. The Bible tells us in Ephesians 6 that Christians are to take up the whole armor of God, and tells us that one of the items we are to use is "the sword of the Spirit, which is the word of God." All Christians, no matter their age, need to read the Bible so they can use it. Some years ago, while working with a children's ministry, I began providing reading sheets to the children to enable them to have a program for reading the Bible. After hearing from parents who appreciated having these sheets for daily devotions with their children, I decided to take it a step further and provide a series of books to enable children to read and understand the Bible.

This book is designed to work with the King James Version, as I believe it to be the most faithful translation currently available in the English language. Other versions of the Bible may work, but may not have the same answers to the questions.

In calculating monetary values throughout this book, I rely on the drachma, or pence. A pence was equal to one days pay to a working man. To calculate this into modern monetary values, I consider $120 to be the average wage of a semi skilled laborer. I base this on eight hours at $15 per hour.

Introduction to Matthew

The Gospel of Matthew was written by the Apostle Matthew Levi. Matthew started as a publican, or tax collector, until Jesus called him to be one of His disciples. Matthew gave up his well paying job collecting taxes for the Romans, and followed Jesus. Very little is said about him in the Bible, other than that he was one of the twelve apostles.

The Gospel of Matthew is one of the three Synoptic, or similar Gospels. It was written sometime between A.D. 50 and A.D. 100. It was likely written primarily for the Jewish believers. Matthew quotes more Old Testament scripture than any of the other Gospels. He shows how Jesus fulfilled all of the prophecies.

Day 1

Read Matthew 1:1-25

Swordfighter's Tip:
When the Bible says that someone "begat" someone else, it means that he is that person's father. The list of people who "begat" other people is called a genealogy. The genealogy in Matthew shows that Jesus is directly related to King David. This gives Him the legal right to rule Israel as her king.

Answer the following questions

1. Who was Jesse's father?

2. How many generations are there from Abraham to David?

3. Who was Mary found with child of?

4. Who appeared to Joseph in a dream?

5. What name means "God with us?"

Day 2

Read Matthew 2:1-23

Swordfighter's Tip:

There are many prophecies in the Bible. A prophecy is where someone says something will happen in the future. Four times this passage mentions prophecies from the Old Testament where prophets said things about how Jesus would be born. These fulfilled prophecies help to show that the other things these prophets wrote were true.

Answer the following questions

1. Where did the wise men come from?

2. Where was Jesus to be born?

3. What three gifts did the wise men give Jesus?

4. Where did Joseph flee with Mary and Jesus?

5. What city did Joseph move to when he left Egypt?

Day 3

Read Matthew 3:1-17

Swordfighter's Tip:
When the Jesus was baptized, a voice from heaven identified Jesus as His Son. This was proof to those around that Jesus was not just a man, He was God who came to earth as a man.

Answer the following questions

1. What did John the Baptist wear?

2. Where did John the Baptist baptize people?

3. What did John the Baptist baptize with?

4. Who came from Galilee to be baptized?

5. What descended like a dove?

 *Fun Fact: John the Baptist was Jesus' second cousin.*

Day 4

Read Matthew 4:1-25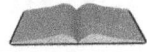

Swordfighter's Tip:

Jesus went more than a month without eating before Satan came to try to get Jesus to sin. Jesus was able to die for our sins because He never sinned. He faced every temptation we will ever face, but even when He was at his weakest, He never sinned. This let Him die for our sins.

Answer the following questions

1. How long did Jesus fast in the wilderness?

2. What did Satan offer Jesus if He would worship Satan?

3. What did Jesus begin to preach?

4. Who did James and John leave to follow Jesus?

5. Where did Jesus' fame go throughout?

Day 5

Read Matthew 5:1-24

Swordfighter's Tip:

When Jesus told people that they needed to exceed the righteousness of the Pharisees, it would have shocked them. The Pharisees appeared to be the most religious people around. What Jesus was saying was that it is not our outward actions that matter the most to God, but who we are on the inside.

Answer the following questions

1. Who shall inherit the earth?

2. Who is the salt of the earth?

3. Where do men put a candle?

4. Whose righteousness do we need to exceed?

5. What is the person who kills in danger of?

Day 6

Read Matthew 5:25-48

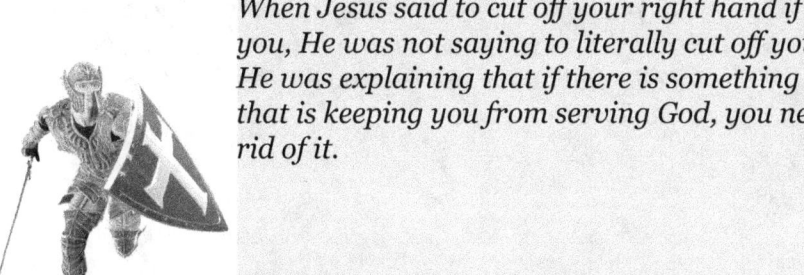

Swordfighter's Tip:
When Jesus said to cut off your right hand if it offends you, He was not saying to literally cut off your hand. He was explaining that if there is something in your life that is keeping you from serving God, you need to get rid of it.

Answer the following questions

1. Who will deliver you to the judge?

2. What are you to do with your right hand?

3. What are you not to swear by?

4. If a man wants your coat, what are you to give also?

5. Who is perfect?

Day 7

Read Matthew 6:1-15

Swordfighter's Tip:
This part of the Bible includes what is called the Lord's Prayer. This is not a prayer we have to recite, but a model of what we are to pray for, and how we ought to pray for it.

Answer the following questions

1. What should we not do before men?

2. Who will reward you openly?

3. What are you not to use when praying?

4. Whose name is hallowed?

5. Who are we to forgive?

Day 8

Read Matthew 6:16-34

Swordfighter's Tip:

Jesus condemned people who made a big deal about their worship in public. Back then, some people would loudly announce how much they were giving in offerings, or would make sure everyone knew they were fasting. Jesus said to worship God privately. God can see what you do in private, and will reward you for it.

Answer the following questions

1. Who disfigure their faces?

2. Where should you not lay up treasure?

3. Who can serve two masters?

4. Who clothes the grass?

5. What should we seek first?

Day 9

Read Matthew 7:1-14

Swordfighter's Tip:
When Jesus said not to judge, He was not saying that we should never say something is not right or wrong, He was saying that we should not hold a person to be of less value than us because of what they do or what they are.

Answer the following questions

1. Why should you not judge?

2. What was in thy brother's eye?

3. What happens to the person who seeketh?

4. If a man's son asks for a fish, what will his father not give him?

5. Which gate are you to enter at?

 Did you know? A mote is a speck of dust.

Day 10

Read Matthew 7:15-29

Swordfighter's Tip:
Jesus warned against false prophets. Not everyone who claims to speak for God does. When you hear someone say God wants you to do something, check to see if what they say agrees with what the Bible says. God already spoke once, and He never changes his mind.

Answer the following questions

1. What clothing do false prophets come in?

2. What does a corrupt tree bring forth?

3. What happens to the tree that doesn't bring forth good fruit?

4. Where did the wise man build his house?

5. Where did the foolish man build his house?

Day 11

Read Matthew 8:1-17

Swordfighter's Tip:
Jesus praised the faith of the centurion. The centurion did not need to see Jesus do great things, he believed Jesus could do great things just by speaking.

Answer the following questions

1. Who asked Jesus to make him clean?

2. What was wrong with the centurion's servant?

3. Who did not believe that he was worthy to have Jesus enter his house?

4. When was the centurion's servant healed?

5. What was wrong with Peter's wife's mother?

 *Fun Fact: Palsy is a disease that paralyses parts of your body.*

Day 12

Read Matthew 8:18-34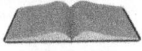

Swordfighter's Tip:
When the disciples were scared of the storm, they had not realized how powerful Jesus is. Because Jesus is God, He can do anything

Answer the following questions

1. What does the Son of man not have?

2. Who did Jesus say to let bury the dead?

3. What did Jesus' disciples follow him into?

4. What did the two men possessed with devils come out of?

5. What did the city want Jesus to do?

Day 13

Read Matthew 9:1-17

Swordfighter's Tip:
When the Bible was written, eating with someone was a big deal. The Pharisees could not understand why Jesus would be friends to those they considered unworthy. When Jesus said not to judge others, He set the example.

Answer the following questions

1. What was the man sick with?

2. Where did the man who was sick go?

3. Who did Jesus tell to follow Him?

4. Who doesn't need a physician?

5. When will the children of the bridegroom mourn?

Day 14

Read Matthew 9:18-38

Swordfighter's Tip:
When Jesus saw the many people who did not believe in Him, He was saddened. He said to pray that God will send people to tell others about Him.

Answer the following questions

1. Who wanted Jesus to heal his daughter?

2. How long was the woman diseased?

3. What did the blind men call Jesus?

4. What did Jesus tell the blind men after He healed them?

5. What is plenteous?

Day 15

Read Matthew 10:1-20

Swordfighter's Tip:

Jesus sent the disciples away from Him to tell others about Him. He sent them out with nothing, promising to supply what they needed when they needed it. Missionaries today go out the same way. They leave to tell others about Jesus, trusting that God will supply what they need.

Answer the following questions

1. Which apostle is called Peter?

2. Which lost sheep were the apostles to go to?

3. What were the apostles do when they entered a house?

4. What were apostles to be wise as?

5. Who would speak in the apostles?

Day 16

Read Matthew 10:21-42

Swordfighter's Tip:

Jesus told the disciples to not think it weird when people didn't like them. When the Pharisees called Jesus "Beelzebub," they were calling Jesus "Satan" If the Pharisees were willing to call Jesus this, they certainly would be willing to attack the disciples. When you tell others about Jesus, don't be surprised if they don't like you.

Answer the following questions

1. Who is not above the master?

2. What were the disciples to speak in light?

3. Who will Jesus confess before the Father?

4. Who will a man's foes be?

5. Who will receive a righteous man's reward?

Day 17

Read Matthew 11:1-15

Swordfighter's Tip:
John the Baptist was the forerunner of Jesus. His job was to tell everyone that Jesus was coming. Jesus will return to earth to take all believers home. We need to tell everyone that Jesus will come again.

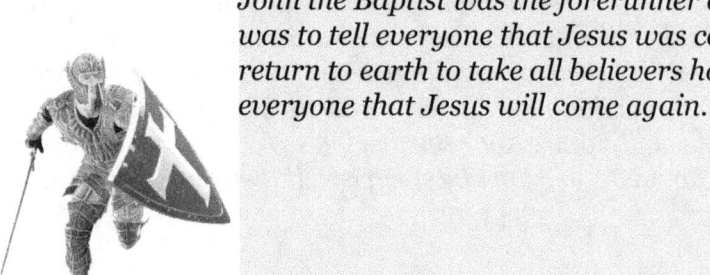

Answer the following questions

1. Where did John hear the works of Christ?

2. Who are cleansed?

3. Where do those who wear soft clothes live?

4. Who prophesied until John?

5. Who is to hear?

Day 18

Read Matthew 11:16-30

Swordfighter's Tip:
Jesus showed the problem with the Jews rejecting His message. They attacked John the Baptist because he didn't eat like normal men. They attacked Jesus because he ate with normal people. In reality, they were rejecting the message because they didn't want to hear it.

Answer the following questions

1. Who are sitting in the markets?

2. How did John come?

3. Where were the mighty works done?

4. Who knows the Son?

5. Whose yoke is easy?

Day 19

Read Matthew 12:1-21

Swordfighter's Tip:

The Old Testament Law forbade working on the Sabbath day, which today we call Saturday. The Pharisees criticized the disciples for picking corn to eat on the Sabbath day. They later criticized Jesus for healing someone on the Sabbath day. Jesus pointed out that the law never forbade helping people or doing what was necessary to survive. The Pharisees had added many rules and exceptions to the law that caused this problem.

Answer the following questions

1. What did the disciples begin to eat?

2. Who is Lord of the Sabbath day?

3. What was wrong with the man's hand?

4. Why did the Pharisees have a counsel about Jesus?

5. In whose name shall the gentiles trust?

Day 20

Read Matthew 12:22-50

Swordfighter's Tip:

This part of the Bible contains what is called the unpardonable (or unforgivable) sin. The Pharisees accused Jesus of being able to work miracles because Satan gave Him power to do so. Jesus warned the Pharisees that this blasphemy (or attack on) of the Holy Spirit would not be forgiven. This was not because God will not forgive this sin, but because when a man has gone so far as to publicly declare that God works miracles through Satan, this man will not accept Jesus.

Answer the following questions

1. Who did they bring to Jesus?

2. How did the Pharisees say Jesus cast out devils?

3. Out of what does the heart speak?

4. Who repented at the preaching of Jonah?

5. Who is Jesus' brother, sister, or mother?

Day 21

Read Matthew 13:1-23

Swordfighter's Tip:

Jesus often taught in what are called parables. A parable is a story told to show a truth. Here, Jesus uses a parable to show how people listen to the Gospel. Some reject it. Some accept it, but when problems come, they stop following Jesus. Some accept it, but soon are busy with everything but serving Jesus. Some accept it and begin serving Jesus.

Answer the following questions

1. What happened to the seeds that fell by the wayside?

2. Which seeds brought forth fruit?

3. What did Esaias say would happen to those who see?

4. Who desired to see and hear what the apostles had seen and heard?

5. What chokes the word?

 ***Did you know?*** *Esaias is another way of spelling Isaiah.*

Day 22

Read Matthew 13:24-58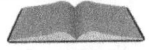

Swordfighter's Tip:
In the parable of the tares (or weeds) of the field, Jesus shows that one day, when He returns, He will sort out those who follow Him from those who reject Him. Those who do not believe in Jesus will then face judgment.

Answer the following questions

1. What did the man sow in the field?

2. What were the reapers to do with the tares?

3. How did Jesus speak to the multitude?

4. What did the merchant sell to get the pearl of great price?

5. Where is a prophet without honour?

Day 23

Read Matthew 14:1-14

Swordfighter's Tip:
Sometimes it isn't easy to tell others the message God has given you. John the Baptist told King Herod that what he was doing was wrong, and Herod didn't like it. Herod put John the Baptist in jail, and then killed him because he did like what John said. Not everybody will react well when we tell them the Gospel, but we need to tell them anyway.

Answer the following questions

1. Who did Herod think was risen from the dead?

2. Who counted John the Baptist a prophet?

3. What did Herodias's daughter ask Herod for?

4. Where did Jesus depart to?

5. What did Jesus do when He saw the multitude?

Day 24

Read Matthew 14:15-36

Swordfighter's Tip:
In this passage, Peter walks on water towards Jesus. While walking on the water, Peter stops looking at Jesus, and starts to look at the storm and the high waves around him. When he begins to doubt what he is doing, he begins to sink. Peter may have briefly doubted what Jesus could do, but he got out of the boat. All of the other disciples stayed in the boat and never put their faith to the test.

Answer the following questions

1. How much food did the disciples have with them?

2. How much remained of the fragments?

3. Where did Jesus go to pray?

4. How did Peter go to Jesus?

5. How many were made whole?

 *Fun Fact: The fourth watch of the night was about 3 a.m.*

Day 25

Read Matthew 15:1-20

Swordfighter's Tip:
Jesus preached against the hypocrisy of the Pharisees. A hypocrite is a person who pretends to be what he is not. The Pharisees pretended to be followers of God, but really they were followers of themselves. They made up rules that let them not have to do what God said. Jesus said that this is wrong. If you want to follow God, you need to do what He says.

Answer the following questions

1. How did the Pharisees say the apostles had transgressed the traditions of the elders?

2. How had the Pharisees made the commandments of God of none effect?

3. What defiles a man?

4. Who shall fall into a ditch?

5. What defileth not a man?

Day 26

Read Matthew 15:21-39

Swordfighter's Tip:

This passage includes the second time Jesus fed a large group of people with very little food. The first time, Jesus fed 5,000 people with five small loaves of bread and two fish. The second time, recorded in this passage Jesus had seven loaves of bread and a few small fish. With this Jesus was able to feed 4,000 men, plus the women and children with them. Jesus is able to, and will provide the needs of those who follow Him.

Answer the following questions

1. Where was the woman from?

2. Which sheep was Jesus sent to?

3. What did the multitudes cast at Jesus' feet?

4. How many loaves did the disciples have?

5. Where did Jesus take a ship to?

Day 27

Read Matthew 16:1-28

Swordfighter's Tip:
When Jesus asked the disciples whom they thought He was, Peter replied that Jesus was God Himself. Jesus at this time gave Peter the name "Peter," which means "little rock." He then used a play on words to tell the apostles, that just as Peter was unmoving in his beliefs, that Christ's church would be built on the large unshakable boulder of the truth that Jesus is God Himself come in human form to pay for our sins.

Answer the following questions

1. What did the Pharisees want Jesus to show them?

2. What did Jesus tell the disciples to beware of?

3. Whom did people say Jesus was?

4. What did Jesus charge the disciples not to tell?

5. How will the Son of man reward every man?

 Did you know? In the Bible, leaven usually stands for sin.

Day 28

Read Matthew 17:1-27

Swordfighter's Tip:

Normally Jesus looked just like another man, but a couple of times, Jesus revealed who He truly was. This was one of those times. Jesus took Peter, James, and John to the top of a mountain, and briefly let His glory shine. When Jesus did this, He showed who He truly is. He is God Himself, sent to earth as a man. Jesus may have been a man, but He was God, with all power and authority.

Answer the following questions

1. Where did Jesus take Peter, James, and John?

2. Who appeared with Jesus on the mountain?

3. What was wrong with the man's son?

4. How much faith did Jesus say the disciples needed?

5. Where did Jesus tell Peter to find the money to pay tribute?

Day 29

Read Matthew 18:1-14

Swordfighter's Tip:
Jesus told His disciples that in order for a person to follow Jesus, they must have faith as a little child. Jesus was referring to the unyielding faith a child has. This can be seen in the unyielding faith a child may have that his dad is the strongest man alive. If you want to believe in Jesus, you must have this unquestioning, unyielding faith in Him.

Answer the following questions

1. What did the disciples ask Jesus?

2. Who is the greatest in the kingdom of heaven?

3. Who receiveth Jesus?

4. Why is the Son of man come?

5. What is not the will of the Father?

Day 30

Read Matthew 18:15-35

Swordfighter's Tip:

When Jesus spoke to the disciples about forgiveness, Peter asked Jesus how many times he should forgive his brother for the same sin. He suggested seven times. Jesus told Peter that seven times was not enough. When Jesus said to forgive your brother seventy times seven, he was not placing a limit on the need to forgive, but rather showing that after you forgive someone for the exact same thing 490 times, you will be willing to forgive always.

Answer the following questions

1. Where did Jesus take Peter, James, and John?

2. Who appeared with Jesus on the mountain?

3. What was wrong with the man's son?

4. How much faith did Jesus say the disciples needed?

5. Where did Jesus tell Peter to find the money to pay tribute?

 *Fun Fact: 10,000 talents equaled about 7.2 billion dollars*

Day 31

Read Matthew 19:1-15

Swordfighter's Tip:

The Pharisees set out trick Jesus by asking Him difficult questions. They wanted people to stop following Jesus. They tried to get Jesus to give the wrong answer to questions, hoping people would stop following Him. Jesus would not be tricked, a gave better answers to the Pharisees every time.

Answer the following questions

1. Where did Jesus go after leaving Galilee?

2. When did God make them male and female?

3. What should man not put asunder?

4. What were brought unto Jesus?

5. Whom did Jesus say to not forbid to come to Him?

Day 32

Read Matthew 19:16-30

Swordfighter's Tip:
When Jesus told the rich young ruler to sell everything he had and follow Jesus, He was not saying that we all have to be poor to serve God, but instead He was showing the ruler that he had not kept the first commandment, to not place anything before God.

Answer the following questions

1. What did the young man call Jesus?

2. Who are you to love as yourself?

3. Why was the young man sorrowful?

4. What is easer than a rich person entering heaven?

5. Who shall receive an hundred fold?

Day 33

Read Matthew 20:1-16

Swordfighter's Tip:

In the parable of the workers in the vineyard, Jesus tells a story of a man who hires a bunch of people to work in his vineyard, promising each man the same amount of money for the day, no matter when he started working that day. Jesus used this to show that those who follow Christ will receive the same reward no matter when they start following Christ.

Answer the following questions

1. How much money did the man offer the workers?

2. What was the third and fourth time the man went to the market to hire workers?

3. How much did those who were hired last get paid?

4. What did the workers who were hired first say?

5. Who shall be first?

 Did you know? A penny was the standard days pay for a working man.

Day 34

Read Matthew 20:17-34

Swordfighter's Tip:
When Jesus told James and John that they would drink of His cup, He was telling them that they would have to face death for Him. All but one of the disciples were killed for telling others about Jesus. We don't have people trying to kill us, so we definitely need to tell others about Jesus.

Answer the following questions

1. Who would the Son of man be betrayed to?

2. Who brought her sons to Jesus?

3. Who has the right to decide who will sit on the left and right hands of Jesus?

4. Why did the Son of man come?

5. What did the blind men call Jesus?

Day 35

Read Matthew 21:1-22

Swordfighter's Tip:
When Jesus attacked the money changers in the Temple, He was attacking the practice they had of requiring everyone to use temple money to buy sacrifices. The money changers would change your money to temple money for a fee. Jesus did not want people to have to pay money just to be able to worship God.

Answer the following questions

1. What did Jesus send the disciples to get?

2. What did the prophet day the King would come riding?

3. What did Jesus call the money changers?

4. Where did Jesus lodge?

5. What shall you receive?

Day 36

Read Matthew 21:23-46

Swordfighter's Tip:

In the parable of two sons, Jesus tells of a father who tells his sons to go work in his fields. One son refuses to go, but later changes his mind and goes. The other son agrees to go, but never does. Jesus uses this to show that Pharisees claimed to follow God, but did not do what God said to do.

Answer the following questions

1. What did Jesus ask the chief priests and elders?

2. What did the people hold John the Baptist to be?

3. What did the householder put in his vineyard?

4. Whom did the householder send to the husbandmen?

5. Why did the Pharisees fear the people?

Day 37

Read Matthew 22:1-22

Swordfighter's Tip:
In the parable of the wedding feast, Jesus shows how some people react when told they need to get saved. Many reject God. They come up with every excuse they can think of. The person cast out for not wearing a wedding garment represents the people who think they can get to heaven by themselves. The host gave out the wedding garments. The person who was not wearing one felt he could get into the wedding on his own.

Answer the following questions

1. Who did the king make a wedding for?

2. Where did those bidden to the wedding go?

3. What did the man at the wedding not have on?

4. Whom did the Pharisees send disciples out with to trap Jesus?

5. What are we to render to Caesar?

Day 38

Read Matthew 22:23-46

Swordfighter's Tip:
When the Pharisees asked Jesus what the greatest commandment was, in addition to trying to trick Jesus, they were trying to solve a debate among themselves. They wanted to know which of their rules was the most important. Jesus did not pick one of the rules of the Pharisees or one of the rules written in the law. He said to love God completely, and care for those around you just like you would care for yourself.

Answer the following questions

1. Who says there is no resurrection?

2. How did the Sadducees err?

3. Who is God the God of?

4. What is the second commandment?

5. Who did the Pharisees say Christ was the son of?

Day 39

Read Matthew 23:1-22

Swordfighter's Tip:

Jesus called out the hypocrisy of the Pharisees, in that they claimed to follow God's laws, but they did not truly obey God. God commanded in the law that widows were to be protected, but the Pharisees would hold public prayers, and then take the widows' houses.

Answer the following questions

1. Where do the scribes sit?

2. What do the Pharisees make their works to be seen of?

3. Who is the one Master?

4. Who shall be exalted?

5. Who sweareth by the throne of God?

Day 40

Read Matthew 23:23-39

Swordfighter's Tip:
Jesus called out the hypocrisy of the Pharisees, showing how they were careful to count out one tenth of everything they owned, down to the tiniest seeds, but they weren't doing the big things like serving God. Jesus said they should be doing both the big and the little.

Answer the following questions

1. What did the Pharisees swallow?

2. What appear beautiful outward?

3. Who are the Pharisees children of?

4. Whom was killed between the temple and the altar?

5. Whose house is left desolate?

Day 41

Read Matthew 24:1-28

Swordfighter's Tip:

When the disciples asked Jesus how they will know when the end times arrive, Jesus gave the disciples several signs to look for. All of these signs are here, and have been here since Jesus left the earth. The next event on God's calendar is when Jesus comes to take us to heaven.

Answer the following questions

1. Where was Jesus when the disciples came to Him?

2. Who will rise against kingdom?

3. What shall be preached in all the world?

4. What should be shortened?

5. What cometh out of the east?

Day 42

Read Matthew 24:29-51

Swordfighter's Tip:

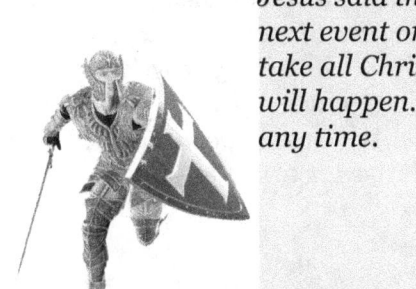

Jesus said that no man knows the day and hour. The next event on God's calendar is when Jesus comes to take all Christians to heaven. No one knows when this will happen. We need to be ready for Him to come at any time.

Answer the following questions

1. When will the sun be darkened?

2. When do we yet know that summer is nigh?

3. Who knows the hour?

4. Who would not have suffered his house to be broken up?

5. What did the evil servant say in his heart?

Day 43

Read Matthew 25:1-28

Swordfighter's Tip:
Jesus gives the example of the lord who went on a journey. Before he left, he gave his servants different amounts of money based on their ability. The faithful servants used their money to make more money, but the unfaithful servant did not. We need to be like the faithful servants and use our abilities for God.

Answer the following questions

1. How many virgins were wise?

2. Where were the foolish virgins when the bridegroom came?

3. How many talents did the man give to the first servant?

4. How many talents did the second servant give his lord?

5. Who did the lord order the unfaithful servant's talent given to?

Day 44

Read Matthew 25:29-46

Swordfighter's Tip:
When Jesus returns to rule this world, He will offer blessings to those who have helped the poor and helpless. He said that those who feed and cloth the needy are feeding and clothing Him.

Answer the following questions

1. Where were they to cast the unprofitable servant?

2. What does the shepherd separate?

3. When did the blessed visit Jesus?

4. When have we fed Jesus?

5. Where will the righteous go?

Day 45

Read Matthew 26:1-35

Swordfighter's Tip:
Jesus tells the disciples exactly what will happen to Him at the Last Supper. He breaks apart a piece of bread and gives to the disciples to show His body will be beaten and broken. He has the disciples drink a cup that represents His blood that He will lose hanging from the cross.

Answer the following questions

1. When did the priests not want to arrest Jesus?

2. What was the ointment in?

3. Which of the twelve went to the chief priests?

4. What did Jesus say was His body?

5. Who would deny Jesus three times?

Day 46

Read Matthew 26:36-56

Swordfighter's Tip:

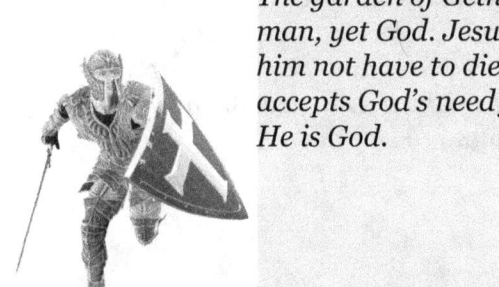

The garden of Gethsemane shows that Jesus was human, yet God. Jesus knelt to pray, and asked God to let him not have to die. This shows He was man. He then accepts God's need for Him to die in agony. This shows He is God.

Answer the following questions

1. What did Jesus ask the disciples to do while He prayed?

2. How did Jesus find the disciples?

3. Who came to arrest Jesus?

4. How did Judah greet Jesus?

5. How many angels did Jesus say God would send Him?

 *Did you know? Twelve legions would be 72,000 angels.*

Day 47

Read Matthew 26:57-75

Swordfighter's Tip:

When the Jewish leaders put Jesus on trial, they tried to get people to lie about Him. God would not let the liars agree. Jewish law required two people to agree in what they say in order to punish someone. All Jesus was convicted of was claiming to be God.

Answer the following questions

1. Who followed Jesus when He was arrested?

2. How long did Jesus say it would take Him to rebuild the temple?

3. What did the high priest say Jesus was guilty of?

4. What did the damsel say to Peter?

5. How many times did Peter deny Jesus?

Day 48

Read Matthew 27:1-31

Swordfighter's Tip:
At the time Jesus was arrested, the Jewish people were not allowed to execute criminals on their own, they had to have the Romans do it. The Jewish leaders brought Jesus to the Roman governor, who offered them a choice. He would either release Jesus who had healed their sick, or he would release Barabbas, a thief and murderer. The Jewish leaders chose Barabbas.

Answer the following questions

1. Who did the chief priests deliver Jesus to?

2. What did the chief priests buy with Judas' money?

3. What was the only thing Jesus said to the governor?

4. Who did the chief priests persuade the multitude to ask for?

5. What did the soldiers put on Jesus?

Day 49

Read Matthew 27:32-66

Swordfighter's Tip:
When the soldiers made Simon of Cyrene to carry the cross of Jesus, they were sending a message. Carrying ones cross then was a sign of guilt. Jesus had no guilt, so He could die for all of our sins.

Answer the following questions

1. What does Golgotha mean?

2. How long was darkness over all the land?

3. What did the centurion say?

4. Who begged the body of Jesus?

5. What did the chief priests do to the sepulcher?

Day 50

Read Matthew 28:1-20

Swordfighter's Tip:

Even though the chief priests put soldiers in front of Jesus' tomb, they could not keep Jesus in the ground. An angel came down, and the soldiers fell to the ground, unconscious. The angel remained at the tomb to let people know that Jesus was not in the tomb, He was alive.

Answer the following questions

1. Who came to the tomb on the first day of the week?

2. Who rolled back the stone from the door?

3. Who met the two ladies as they went to tell the disciples?

4. What did the elders tell the soldiers to say?

5. Who is with us alway?

Introduction to Mark

The Gospel of Mark was likely written by John Mark. Like most of the writers of scripture, little is know about John Mark from the Bible. He was young man who lived in Jerusalem. It was likely at his house that Jesus held the last supper. He briefly traveled with the Apostle Paul and Barnabas, until he abandoned him in the middle of a trip. He then traveled with Barnabas, with Paul splitting off to go with Silas. Eventually, Paul came to accept Mark, pronouncing him fit for the ministry in one of his last letters.

The Gospel of Mark may have been the first Gospel written, sometime between A.D. 50 and A.D. 70. Along with Matthew and Luke it is one of the Synoptic, or similar Gospels. These three books share a lot in common. Almost all other writers from the early church believed that Mark wrote his Gospel to the Christians in Rome. It is the shortest Gospel, focusing on the works of Jesus, and the failures of the disciples.

Day 51

Read Mark 1:1-20

Swordfighter's Tip:
The Trinity is a doctrine that can be hard to understand. How can one person be three people. his passage shows all three at once. When Jesus, God's son was coming out of the water, God the Holy Spirit came down like a dove, and God the Father spoke from heaven. The Trinity is not one God with three jobs, but one God who is three beings.

Answer the following questions

1. What did the voice in the wilderness cry?

2. What did John eat?

3. What did Jesus see Simon and Andrew doing?

4. What did Jesus say He would make Simon and Andrew?

5. Who was James' father?

Day 52

Read Mark 1:21-45

Swordfighter's Tip:
The Old Testament told the Jews to watch for those who could do miracles like healing people. This was a sign they were sent from God. Jesus did more than the prophets of the Old Testament were able to do. This is what amazed the Jews, and should have told them to believe Him.

Answer the following questions

1. What did Jesus tell the man with the unclean spirit?

2. Who lay sick of the fever?

3. Where did Jesus go in the morning?

4. Where did Jesus preach?

5. What did Jesus tell the leper not to do?

Day 53

Read Mark 2:1-17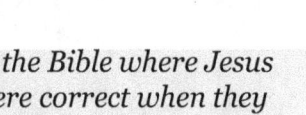

Swordfighter's Tip:
This is one of the many parts of the Bible where Jesus claims to be God. The scribes were correct when they said that only God can forgive sin. Jesus demonstrated He had that power by healing the man.

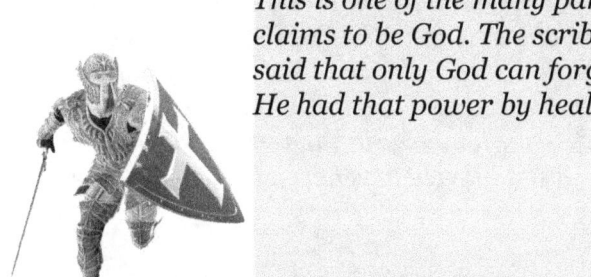

Answer the following questions

1. Who did the four men bring to Jesus?

2. What did Jesus first say to the sick man?

3. What did the scribes reason in their hearts?

4. Where did Jesus find Levi?

5. Whom did Jesus come to call to repentance?

Day 54

Read Mark 2:18-28

Swordfighter's Tip:
The Pharisees fasted, or went without eating a lot. The people who followed John the Baptist did so as well. The Pharisees asked Jesus why His disciples did not fast. Jesus said that because He was with them, there was no need to fast. After Jesus left the earth, His disciples would fast, but while He was here, there was no need to fast.

Answer the following questions

1. Who fasted not?

2. What do people not sew on an old garment?

3. What did Jesus' disciples pluck in the field?

4. What did David do in the days of Abiathar?

5. Who is Lord of the Sabbath?

Day 55

Read Mark 3:1-21

Swordfighter's Tip:
Jesus was not some perfectly calm person. He saw how the Pharisees had made a bunch of rules that ignored the meaning of the Law and got angry. He healed a man on the Sabbath day to show they were wrong.

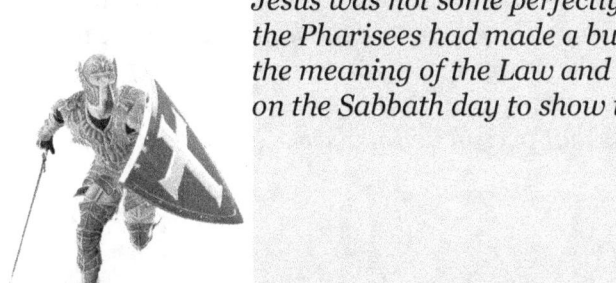

Answer the following questions

1. Who was in the synagogue?

2. Who did the Pharisees take counsel with?

3. Who pressed to touch Jesus?

4. What did Jesus name James and John?

5. Who betrayed Jesus?

Day 56

Read Mark 3:22-35

Swordfighter's Tip:
In an attempt to discredit Jesus' ability to cast out demons, scribes, or teachers of the Law, claimed that He did so by the power of Satan. Jesus said that if a person goes so far as to claim that God's work was done by Satan, than that person will not seek God's forgiveness.

Answer the following questions

1. How did the scribes say Jesus cast out devils?

2. What house cannot stand?

3. What will be forgiven the sons of men?

4. Who came to seek Jesus?

5. Who did Jesus say is His brother?

Day 57

Read Mark 4:1-20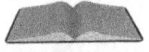

Swordfighter's Tip:
Jesus often taught in parables, or stories. These stories were used to illustrate a point He was making. Sometimes He explained the meaning behind the parable. Here He tells the parable of the sower. He uses this story to show how different people react when they hear His message.

Answer the following questions

1. Who went out to sow?

2. What choked up the seed?

3. Who should hear?

4. What does the sower sow?

5. What do the thorns represent?

Day 58

Read Mark 4:21-41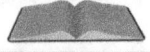

Swordfighter's Tip:

Jesus compares the kingdom of God to four things, a candle, to show we need to tell others about it, a measurement to show that we will be judged for what we do, a sower to show that we don't understand how God works, and a mustard seed to show that even the least gifted can be used by God to accomplish great things.

Answer the following questions

1. What is a candle not put under?

2. What shall be measured to you?

3. What is less than all the seeds in the earth?

4. Where was Jesus in the ship?

5. Who do the wind and sea obey?

Day 59

Read Mark 5:1-21

Swordfighter's Tip:
Why did Jesus allow the devils to kill the pigs? The Jews were not allowed to eat anything from pigs. They were raising them to sell to others who didn't follow the law. God does not approve of us helping others to do what we know to be wrong.

Answer the following questions

1. What had been plucked asunder?

2. What was the unclean spirit's name?

3. How many pigs were there?

4. How did they find the man who had been possessed?

5. Where did the man tell what Jesus had done for him?

Day 60

Read Mark 5:22-43

Swordfighter's Tip:

Jesus often said that people who had died were sleeping. He said this because death is not the end, but a doorway to eternity. Jesus multiple times raised people from the dead, showing that He is the master of life and death.

Answer the following questions

1. How long had the woman been sick?

2. What did the sick woman want to do to Jesus?

3. Who did Jesus allow to follow Him to the house?

4. What did Jesus say to the girl?

5. How old was the girl?

Day 61

Read Mark 6:1-29

Swordfighter's Tip:
When Jesus tried to preach to the people where He grew up, they wouldn't listen. The only cared about where He was from and who His parents were, not the message He had to say. It is important to remember that God can use anyone, regardless of where they were born, or who their family is.

Answer the following questions

1. Where is a prophet without honor?

2. What were the disciples to take with them on their journey?

3. Who did Herod say Jesus was?

4. Why did Herod fear John the Baptist?

5. What did Herodias' daughter demand from Herod?

Day 62

Read Mark 6:30-56

Swordfighter's Tip:

In the time Jesus lived, a working man earned one penny a day. When Jesus told the disciples to feed the crowd, they tried to show Jesus how impossible it would be, saying they would need 200 pennies, or 25,000 to 30,000 dollars in today's money just to buy bread to feed the crowd. They forgot what Jesus could do with what the crowd had.

Answer the following questions

1. What had the disciples not had the leisure to do?

2. Why was Jesus moved with compassion?

3. How many loaves did the disciples bring to Jesus?

4. How many baskets were left over?

5. What time did Jesus go out on the water to the disciples?

Day 63

Read Mark 7:1-23

Swordfighter's Tip:

Jesus called out the Pharisees on their hypocrisy. They twisted the law to their own ends. Jesus gives one example of how they had twisted the law. The Law commanded a person to take care of his parents when they got old. The Pharisees created an exception to this. They declared all of their money to be "Corban" or "given to God." They would then tell their parents they couldn't help them because all of their money belonged to God.

Answer the following questions

1. What did the Pharisees find fault with the disciples?

2. What did Esaias prophecy about the Pharisees?

3. What did the Pharisees make the word of God?

4. What defiles a man?

5. What proceeds out of the heart?

Day 64

Read Mark 7:24-37

Swordfighter's Tip:
Jesus chose to engage in word play with the Syrophencian woman to show what was wrong with some of the Jewish beliefs at that time. The Jews called the Gentiles "Dogs," and considered them to be of lower value. Jesus showed that even the Gentiles were worthy of His help.

Answer the following questions

1. What borders did Jesus go into?

2. What did the woman want Jesus to do?

3. Where did the woman find her daughter?

4. What did Jesus tell the deaf man?

5. Who did they say Jesus made to hear?

Day 65

Read Mark 8:1-21

Swordfighter's Tip:
When the Pharisees asked Jesus for a sign, they would claim they were following the Law. The Law said that those who claimed to be from God would be given the ability to do miracles to prove they were sent by God. The Pharisees were ignoring all the miracles Jesus had done. That is why Jesus told them there would be no sign. No matter what Jesus did, they wouldn't believe Him.

Answer the following questions

1. How long had the multitude been with Jesus?

2. How many loaves did they have?

3. What did the Pharisees ask Jesus for?

4. What had the disciples forgotten to take?

5. How many baskets of leftovers were gathered up from the four thousand?

Day 66

Read Mark 8:22-38

Swordfighter's Tip:

Jesus began to teach His closest followers what would happen to Him. He would be rejected, die and yet rise from the dead. Peter couldn't understand this, believing that Jesus could do anything. He couldn't see that Jesus had to die to pay for our sins.

Answer the following questions

1. What did Jesus ask His disciples?

2. Who must suffer many things?

3. Who began to rebuke Jesus?

4. What does the person who will follow Jesus need to take up?

5. For whom will the Son of man be ashamed?

Day 67

Read Mark 9:1-29

Swordfighter's Tip:
When Jesus was transfigured in front of Peter, James, and John, He for just a little while revealed His full power and glory. It is hard for us to understand, but Jesus was completely human, but also completely God. Because Jesus was completely human, He could face every temptation we will ever face. Because He was completely God, He could live without sin. This was the only way He could become the perfect sacrifice.

Answer the following questions

1. Who did Jesus take to the mountain?

2. Who appeared with Jesus?

3. Who did the scribes say must first come?

4. What did the father ask Jesus to help him with?

5. Why could the disciples, not cast out the demon?

Day 68

Read Mark 9:30-50

Swordfighter's Tip:
When Jesus said that a person should cut off his hand if it offended him, He was not saying you should literally chop off your hand. He was saying that if something you enjoy doing is keeping you from following God, you should get rid of it.

Answer the following questions

1. When shall the Son of man rise?

2. Who shall be the last?

3. Who is on our part?

4. Where is the fire that shall never be quenched?

5. Who were the disciples to have peace with?

Day 69

Read Mark 10:1-31

Swordfighter's Tip:

When Jesus said that one must receive the kingdom of God as a little child, He was referring to their absolute and total faith. Just as a little child is certain that his daddy is the strongest, toughest man alive, so too must we believe that Jesus died for our sins and rose again.

Answer the following questions

1. What did God make from the beginning of creation?

2. What should man not put asunder?

3. Who is good?

4. What did Jesus tell the man that he lacked?

5. With whom are all things possible?

Day 70

Read Mark 10:32-52

Swordfighter's Tip:

Jesus explained an important rule for His followers to the disciples. Just as Jesus did not come to sit on a throne, but instead came to die for all men, so to are Christian leaders supposed to lead from an attitude of service. They are not to rule over believers, but to do what is best for others with no thought for themselves.

Answer the following questions

1. Where did Jesus say they were going?

2. What did James and John ask Jesus?

3. What did the Son of man come for?

4. Who sat by the highway begging?

5. What did Jesus say had made the man whole?

Day 71

Read Mark 11:1-19

Swordfighter's Tip:

When Jesus lived, the Jews were required to pay a tax at the temple every year. They were required to use a particular coin to pay the tax. The moneychangers would change your money to these coins for a large price. That is why Jesus called them thieves. God does not want people to get rich just so that others can worship Him.

Answer the following questions

1. What did Jesus send the disciples to get?

2. What did the disciples put on the colt?

3. Where did Jesus go for the eventide?

4. What did Jesus overthrow?

5. Why did the chief priests fear Jesus?

Day 72

Read Mark 11:20-33

Swordfighter's Tip:
When Jesus said that if you have faith in God, you can command a mountain to be thrown into the ocean, He was referring to the source of the Christian's power. For a Christian to do anything in life, he must believe that God can do it. When he prays for God to do something, he must believe that God is able to do it.

Answer the following questions

1. What was withered away?

2. What must one do when he prays?

3. Who came to Jesus in the temple?

4. What question did Jesus ask the scribes?

5. What did all men count John to be?

Day 73

Read Mark 12:1-27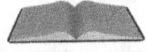

Swordfighter's Tip:

Jesus uses a story to show one of the problems with the Pharisees. First, God sent prophets to correct Israel, but the Jews rejected the prophets. Now God has sent His Son, but the Pharisees were so caught up in their traditions, they were planning to kill God's son because He spoke against their rules and traditions.

Answer the following questions

1. What did the husbandmen do to the second servant?

2. What is become the head of the corner?

3. What are we to render to Caesar?

4. Who says there is no resurrection?

5. Who is God the God of?

Day 74

ReadMark 12:28-44

Swordfighter's Tip:

After Jesus avoided all the traps the religious leaders set for Him, one of the teachers asked Jesus to settle a debate about what was the most important commandment. Jesus responded that the most important commandment is to put God first in everything, and secondly to care as much for others as you care for yourself. If you do these things, you will have no trouble obeying the law.

Answer the following questions

1. What did the scribe ask Jesus?

2. What is more than burnt offerings?

3. Who do the scribes say Christ is?

4. What do the scribes love to go in?

5. What did the widow cast into the treasury?

Day 75

Read Mark 13:1-23

Swordfighter's Tip:

When the one of the disciples praised the beauty of the temple, Jesus said that the day would come that one stone would not stand on another. This happened in A.D. 70, when the Roman soldiers burned the city of Jerusalem. The fires from the city melted all the gold on the temple, and the Roman soldiers ripped the stones apart to get the gold. When Jesus promises something will happen, it will happen.

Answer the following questions

1. Why should we take heed?

2. What shall rise against nation?

3. Who shall be saved?

4. For what should the man in the field not turn back?

5. Who shall rise?

Day 76

Read Mark 13:24-37

Swordfighter's Tip:
Jesus said that just as even though you may not know exactly when summer will start, you can get an idea by looking at the leaves on a tree. Just the same, you can know something about when Jesus will come back by watching the signs of the times. Everything that Jesus said needs to happen before He comes back has happened. We need to live our lives as if Jesus could come back any minute.

Answer the following questions

1. What shall not give her light?

2. From where shall he gather His elect?

3. What shall not pass until all this be fulfilled?

4. Who knows the hour?

5. What does Jesus say unto all?

Day 77

Read Mark 14:1-21

Swordfighter's Tip:

Part of the method the Jews used to bury the dead in Jesus' time involved pouring good smelling oils on the body. Jesus knew that because of the Passover, they would not be able to properly bury Him. That is why Jesus said that the woman anointed Him for His burial.

Answer the following questions

1. What was after two days?

2. How much could the ointment be sold for?

3. When did they kill the passover?

4. What would they find a man bearing?

5. What is good for the man who betrays the Son of man?

 *Did you know? 300 pence is about $36,000.*

Day 78

Read Mark 14:22-45

Swordfighter's Tip:

In churches today we eat bread and drink grape juice just like the disciples did at the last supper. He told the disciples that the bread represented His body which was injured for them, and the juice represented His blood which was shed for them. We eat the same things today because God commanded us to, to help us remember what Jesus did for us.

Answer the following questions

1. What do we not war after?

2. What are we to bring into captivity?

3. What did the Apostle Paul not want to seem to terrify the Corinthians by?

4. Who are not wise?

5. Who is approved?

Day 79

Read Mark 14:46-72

Swordfighter's Tip:

When Jesus said "Ye took me not," He was telling the guards who arrested Him that they had no power to arrest Jesus, but He was willing to go with them to pay for our sins. No one made Jesus go to the cross, He willingly died for us.

Answer the following questions

1. What did the man with the sword cut off?

2. Who was with the High Priest?

3. What did the false witnesses say Jesus would destroy?

4. Who saw Peter beneath in the palace?

5. What word had Jesus said to Peter?

Day 80

Read Mark 15:1-28

Swordfighter's Tip:

Who was Barabbas? We know very little about him. We don't even know his name. Barabbas just means son of his father. We know he had committed murder. John tells us that he was a thief. He had tried to lead an uprising against Rome, but had failed. He was waiting to be executed for his crimes, when Pilate, trying to save the life of Jesus, offered to release him. Just as Jesus took Barabbas' place on the cross, so He takes our place on the cross, paying for our sins.

Answer the following questions

1. Who did the chief priests deliver Jesus to?

2. What had Barabbas committed?

3. What did the soldiers cloth Jesus with?

4. Who was the father of Alexander?

5. What was written on the superscription?

Day 81

Read Mark 15:29-47

Swordfighter's Tip:
When Jesus died, the veil in the temple was torn in two. This veil separated the Holy of Holies in the temple from the Holy Place where the priests would offer incense. The Holy of Holies held the Ark of the Covenant, which signified God's presence. When God tore the veil in two, He signified that no longer did men need to go through a priest to get to God, they could call upon Him on their own now that the price of sin was paid.

Answer the following questions

1. What happened on the sixth hour?

2. What did they offer Jesus to drink?

3. What did the centurion say about Jesus?

4. Who asked Pilate for the body of Jesus?

5. Who beheld where the body of Jesus was laid?

Day 82

Read Mark 16:1-20

Swordfighter's Tip:

Because Jesus was buried right before the sabbath day, or Saturday, the people who buried Him could not do the job properly. The Jews were not allowed to do any work on the sabbath day, so Mary and Mary Magdalene went to the tomb early on Sunday morning when the sabbath was over to finish the job. There they found Jesus' body gone, and an angel telling them that Jesus had risen from the dead.

Answer the following questions

1. What day of the week did the ladies go to the tomb?

2. Who did they see in the sepulcher?

3. Who did Jesus appear to first?

4. When did Jesus appear to the eleven?

5. Where did the disciples preach?

Introduction to Luke

The Gospel of Luke was likely written by Luke, a Gentile doctor. It is noteworthy that Luke was the only Gentile to write a book of the Bible. He wrote both the Gospel of Luke and the book of Acts. Luke was a Gentile, also called a physician, or doctor. Luke traveled with the Apostle Paul during his later journeys.

The Gospel of Luke was probably the last of the Synoptic, or similar Gospels written. Luke writes to a man called Theophilus, or friend of God. Theophilus was likely a government official who either was a Christian or wanted to become one. The Gospel of Luke is the longest Gospel, primarily written to show how the Christian faith came to be. Luke writes a lot about salvation and deliverance in his Gospel.

Day 83

Read Luke 1:1-25

Swordfighter's Tip:

We don't know how old Zacharias was when John was born, just that he and Elizabeth were very old. Zacharias asked the angel for a sign that what he promised would happen. This is what God had told the Jews to do in the Old Testament. Zacharias wanted to make sure that it was an angel from God telling him these things, so he asked the angel for a sign.

Answer the following questions

1. Who did Luke write to?

2. What did Zacharias execute?

3. What was Zacharias to name his son?

4. What was the angel's name?

5. How long did Elizabeth hide herself?

Day 84

Read Luke 1:26-45

Swordfighter's Tip:

One essential part of the story of Jesus is that He was born of a virgin. When the angel Gabriel came to Mary, it says multiple times that she was a virgin. This was important because Isaiah had written that Jesus would be born of a virgin. Every part of how Jesus came into this world was miraculous.

Answer the following questions

1. In what month did Gabriel come to Mary?

2. Whose throne would be given to Jesus?

3. Who was called barren?

4. What city did Mary go to?

5. Who was filled with the Holy Ghost?

Day 85

Read Luke 1:46-66

Swordfighter's Tip:

When the time came to name the baby John the Baptist, the family members around could not believe that Elizabeth would name the child John. Zacharias had no family members by that name, and children were usually named after someone in their line. When Zacharias wrote that the child was named John, he was able to speak again.

Answer the following questions

1. Who is God's mercy on?

2. How long did Mary stay with Elizabeth?

3. What did they want to name the baby?

4. What did Zacharias write?

5. When was Zacharias' mouth opened?

Day 86

Read Luke 1:67-80

Swordfighter's Tip:

When John the Baptist was born, his father under the control of the Holy Spirit announced to everyone around that John would be the forerunner of Jesus. Isaiah had prophesied that there would be someone who would come to earth before the Messiah. He would proclaim that the Messiah was coming. John the Baptist was this person. He lived in the desert, and proclaimed that the Messiah was coming.

Answer the following questions

1. Who was Zacharias filled with?

2. What hath God raised up in the house of David?

3. Who did God swear the oath to?

4. What shall the child be called?

5. What did the child wax strong in?

Day 87

Read Luke 2:1-20

Swordfighter's Tip:

When Caesar Augustus sent out the command to count everyone in the empire, in order to more fairly charge taxes, he had no idea that he would help fulfill a prophecy. The prophet Micah had written that the Messiah would be born in Bethlehem, but Mary and Joseph lived in Nazareth. They would have to travel to Bethlehem, because all of the descendants of David had to go there.

Answer the following questions

1. Who was governor of Syria?

2. Who was Joseph of the lineage of?

3. Where would the shepherds find the babe?

4. What did the shepherds find?

5. What did the shepherds praise God for?

Day 88

Read Luke 2:21-35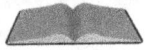

Swordfighter's Tip:
Everything about Jesus' birth was special. When His parents took Him to the temple shortly after He was born to present him to God, a man named Simon was there. Simon was very old, but had been told by God that he would see the Messiah before he died. When Mary and Joseph brought Jesus in, Simon knew that God had fulfilled His promise.

Answer the following questions

1. Where was the child brought?

2. What sacrifice did Mary and Joseph need to offer?

3. Where did Simon go by the Spirit?

4. What had Simon's eyes seen?

5. What did Joseph marvel at?

Day 89

Read Luke 2:36-52

Swordfighter's Tip:
For the feast of Passover, every Jewish person who was able to travel, would go to Jerusalem to celebrate the feast. This is why it was easy for Mary and Joseph to miss Jesus when they first left to go home, because they thought he might have been with one of their relatives. Every single member of Jesus family was traveling in one big group to go home.

Answer the following questions

1. Who was the prophetess?

2. What was Mary and Joseph's own city?

3. What was the child filled with?

4. Who tarried behind in Jerusalem?

5. Who was Jesus subject to?

Day 90

Read Luke 3:1-18

Swordfighter's Tip:

John the Baptist gets his name because he baptized people who followed him. This baptism was merely an outward sign to others that a person had repented and wanted to follow God. That is what baptism is today. It is not a requirement of salvation, but rather an sign to others who see it that we have chosen to follow God.

Answer the following questions

1. Who was governor of Judea?

2. Who were the high priests?

3. Who shall see the salvation of God?

4. What did John the Baptist say to the publicans?

5. What did John baptize with?

Day 91

Read Luke 3:19-58

Swordfighter's Tip:

Who someone's ancestors were was very important to the Jewish people. Luke tells the genealogy of Mary in his Gospel. Because the seed of woman would break the curse of sin, Luke shows who Mary came from down to David, and even on to Adam and Eve. This was to show that God would keep all His promises.

Answer the following questions

1. What descended from heaven?

2. Who was the son of Sem-e-i?

3. Who was the son of Jo-rim?

4. Who was the son of David?

5. Who was the son of Enoch?

Day 92

Read Luke 4:1-15

Swordfighter's Tip:

When Satan came to tempt Jesus, Jesus was extremely weak. He had not eaten anything for over one month. Most of us will never have Satan come to us directly to tempt us. If Jesus could at his weakest resist temptation by quoting the Bible, then we can face what temptations come at us.

Answer the following questions

1. Where did Jesus return from?

2. How many days was Jesus tempted of the devil?

3. What shall man live by?

4. Where did Satan take Jesus to in Jerusalem?

5. Where did Jesus teach in?

Day 93

Read Luke 4:16-30

Swordfighter's Tip:
When Jesus went to teach in Nazareth, the people there did not want to believe Him. They saw Him as only Joseph's son, whom they had seen grow up. When Jesus showed them that quite often the prophets in Israel were not able to work miracles because people did not want believe in them, the people grew angry. We need to listen to what God's teachers say before we think about who their parent's are.

Answer the following questions

1. What book was brought to Jesus?

2. Who did Jesus give the book to?

3. Who did the people say was Jesus' father?

4. Where was Elias sent?

5. Where did the crowd take Jesus?

Day 94

Read Luke 4:31-44

Swordfighter's Tip:
Jesus would not let the demons possessing people say who He was because people knew that they lied. Jesus knew that the truth cannot come from a source that is proven to be untrustworthy.

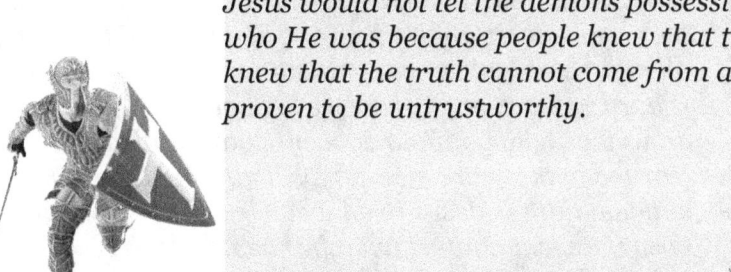

Answer the following questions

1. What city did Jesus come to?

2. Who cried out with a loud voice?

3. Where did Jesus fame go?

4. Whose house did Jesus enter?

5. Where did Jesus go when He left the city?

Day 95

Read Luke 5:1-15

Swordfighter's Tip:

When Jesus told Simon to put his nets in the water, Simon was uncertain. He knew he had been on the water all night and had not caught anything. He knew that it is hard to catch any fish in the heat of the day, so what Jesus was telling him to do went against all he had learned in his years making his living catching fish. He still had faith in Jesus to do what Jesus asked of him, even if it went against what he knew.

Answer the following questions

1. What lake did Jesus stand by?

2. Whose ship did Jesus enter?

3. What happened when Simon put the net in the water?

4. What was Simon Peter astonished at?

5. What did the multitudes come for?

Day 96

Read Luke 5:16-39

Swordfighter's Tip:
Publicans were tax collectors. They were known for cheating people and overcharging them on their taxes, so they could get rich. The Pharisees could not understand why Jesus would spend time with them, because they weren't good people. Jesus told them that He had come not to help those who were righteous, but instead to get sinners to turn to God.

Answer the following questions

1. What was wrong with the man on the bed?

2. Who can forgive sins?

3. Who hath power on earth to forgive sins?

4. What was the name of the publican?

5. What must new wine be put in?

Day 97

Read Luke 6:1-19

Swordfighter's Tip:
When the disciples were with Jesus, they were seen picking some ears of corn from a field on the Sabbath day. The law forbade the Jews from work on the Sabbath day, and the Pharisees had come up with a lot of special rules. They did not understand that Jesus and His disciples were willing to follow God's laws, but not the rules the Pharisees had come up with.

Answer the following questions

1. What did the disciples eat?

2. Who is Lord of the Sabbath?

3. Why did the Pharisees watch Jesus?

4. Where did Jesus go to pray?

5. Who was Simon's brother?

Day 98

Read Luke 6:20-49

Swordfighter's Tip:
Jesus told His disciples to do what was not expected. He told them to step above how people behave, and love those who attack them. Jesus did this Himself, when He willingly went to the cross for us. We are told to do what Jesus did.

Answer the following questions

1. Whose is the kingdom of God?

2. What should we do to those who hate us?

3. Who is merciful?

4. What does a good tree not bring forth?

5. What is a man who hears and does not like?

Day 99

Read Luke 7:1-18

Swordfighter's Tip:

Jesus was amazed by the faith shown by the centurion, a commander in the Roman army. The centurion had a servant who got very sick. He sent people to ask Jesus to heal the servant. When he heard Jesus was coming, he sent people to tell Jesus He didn't need to come. He said as an officer, he could command soldiers, and he knew that Jesus could just speak and command his servant to be healed.

Answer the following questions

1. Where did Jesus enter?

2. What had the centurion built?

3. What did Jesus say to the woman?

4. Who sat up?

5. Where did the rumor spread?

Day 100

Read Luke 7:19-35

Swordfighter's Tip:

John the Baptist was chosen to be the forerunner of Jesus. When he heard of Jesus' miracles, he sent people to ask if Jesus was the one who he was sent to tell everyone of. Jesus performed many miracles in front of them, and sent them back to John to tell what they saw. Just as John the Baptist was sent to tell people that Jesus was coming, so we need to tell people that Jesus came.

Answer the following questions

1. How many people did John send?

2. Who is blessed?

3. Who are in the kings courts?

4. Who rejected the counsel of God?

5. Who is justified of all her children?

 *Did you know? Jesus quoted Malachi 3:4.*

Day 101

Read Luke 7:36-50

Swordfighter's Tip:

One of the Pharisees invited Jesus to eat with him. At that time, it was customary to have a servant wash the grime off a persons feet when they entered a house. He did not do this for Jesus. When the Pharisee questioned in his mind why Jesus would let a known sinner close to Him, Jesus reminded the Pharisee that he had not done this for Jesus, but a person who knew how much she had gained from Him had washed His feet with her tears.

Answer the following questions

1. What did the woman bring?

2. What was the Pharisee's name?

3. How much did the first debtor owe?

4. What did Simon not give Jesus for his feet?

5. What had saved the woman?

Day 102

Read Luke 8:1-18

Swordfighter's Tip:
When Jesus spoke in parables, or stories, He did not always explain himself to the crowd. When He said, "He that hath an ear, let him hear," He was saying that to those who truly wanted to follow God, God would give the meaning. Because He was with the disciples, He told the meaning to them.

Answer the following questions

1. Out of whom came seven devils?

2. Where were people come to Jesus from?

3. How much fruit did the seed which fell on good ground bring?

4. What are they which fell on a rock?

5. Where does a man not put a candle?

Day 103

Read Luke 8:19-40

Swordfighter's Tip:
Because Jesus was the oldest son in His family, when Joseph died, His brothers brought Mary to Him because the Law demanded the oldest son take care of his parents when they got old, in exchange for a double portion of his inheritance. Jesus took no inheritance, and explained that He had fully left His family in order to minister to Israel.

Answer the following questions

1. Out of whom came seven devils?

2. Where were people come to Jesus from?

3. How much fruit did the seed which fell on good ground bring?

4. What are they which fell on a rock?

5. Where does a man not put a candle?

Day 104

Read Luke 8:41-56

Swordfighter's Tip:

While Jesus was on his way to heal the girl, a woman who had been sick for most of her life touched Him. She had consulted every doctor, but no one had been able to help her. In desperation, she believed that if she could just touch Jesus, she would be healed. When Jesus knew she had touched Him, He told her that her faith in Him had healed her.

Answer the following questions

1. What was Jairus in charge of?

2. How old was Jairus' daughter?

3. How long had the woman had the issue of blood?

4. Who went with Jesus into the house?

5. What did Jesus tell the daughter?

Day 105

Read Luke 9:1-17

Swordfighter's Tip:

When King Herod heard about what Jesus was doing, he was confused. There was no internet or television back then. The only way news traveled was by what people said. By the time the news got to Herod, people were telling him that John the Baptist was doing these things. Herod had already had John killed, so he knew it wasn't him. He just wanted to find out who Jesus was.

Answer the following questions

1. What did Jesus give His disciples power over?

2. Who was told to Herod to have risen from the dead?

3. Where did the desert place belong to?

4. How many people were supposed to sit in a company?

5. How many baskets of fragments were gathered?

Day 106

Read Luke 9:18-45

Swordfighter's Tip:

Many people did not know who Jesus was when He lived. Some people thought Jesus was Elijah returned from the dead. Other people thought He must be a great prophet, like had been seen in the Old Testament. They were excited, because it had been 400 years since God had sent a prophet to Israel. The disciples were the first to see that Jesus was not just a prophet, He was God come to earth.

Answer the following questions

1. Who did people say Jesus was?

2. Who must the Son of man be rejected of?

3. How many days passed before Jesus took Pete, James, and John to the mountain?

4. What did the voice from the cloud say?

5. Who could not cast out the spirit?

Day 107

Read Luke 9:46-62

Swordfighter's Tip:
John saw someone working miracles in God's name, but he told him to stop. John thought that only those who traveled with Jesus should be able to work miracles. Jesus told John that whoever was not working against Him was working for Him. Jesus knew that only someone who truly believed in Jesus could do what this man was seen doing.

Answer the following questions

1. What reasoning rose amongst the disciples?

2. Where did Jesus set His face to?

3. What is the Son of man come to do?

4. What does the Son of man not have?

5. Who should bury the dead?

Day 108

Read Luke 10:1-20

Swordfighter's Tip:
When Jesus sent out the seventy disciples, He told them to take nothing with them. He wanted them to entirely live off what people gave them. He said the labourer is worthy of his payment. To often people forget that God wants Christians to support those who minister to them, as they are working for the Lord.

Answer the following questions

1. How many disciples did Jesus send in each group?

2. What are few?

3. What were the disciples to eat in each city?

4. What city was exalted to heaven?

5. Why should the disciples rejoice?

Day 109

Read Luke 10:21-42

Swordfighter's Tip:

The lawyer wanted to test Jesus and trip Him up when he asked how to get eternal life. He knew what Jesus said the greatest commandment was, but he wanted to have things his own way when he asked Jesus who his neighbor was. At that time, the Jews hated the Samaritans, who were only part Jewish. It was so bad that they would go out of their way to avoid going through Samaria. Jesus knew this when He showed that God sees everyone around us as our neighbors.

Answer the following questions

1. Who had desired to see what the disciples saw?

2. Who stood up and tempted Jesus?

3. Where was the man traveling?

4. How much money did the Samaritan give to take care of the wounded man?

5. What had Mary chosen?

Day 110

Read Luke 11:1-26

Swordfighter's Tip:
When Jesus said, "Ask and ye shall receive," it must be understood in harmony with other scripture. God will not just give us everything we ask for. This passage makes clear that God wants to give us good and helpful things, but the Bible also talks about praying in God's will. When we ask God for things that are in His will for us to have, He will grant them to us.

Answer the following questions

1. What did one of Jesus' disciples ask Him?

2. Why will the friend rise up and give the loaves?

3. Who receiveth?

4. Who is against Jesus?

5. What is worst than the first?

Day 111

Read Luke 11:27-54

Swordfighter's Tip:

Jonah was sent to Ninevah with a simple message. Turn back to God or be destroyed. Jesus was sent with the same message. Other nations would judge Israel, because they refused to turn back to God. Ninevah had turned to God when Jonah preached to them, but Israel would not accept Jesus' message.

Answer the following questions

1. What was Jonah a sign to?

2. Where does a man put a candle?

3. Who besought Jesus to dine with them?

4. What did the Pharisees love?

5. What had the lawyers taken away?

Day 112

Read Luke 12:1-21

Swordfighter's Tip:
Jesus cautions us about focusing on what is on earth. He told the story of a rich man who looked at his wealth, and decided to build bigger storehouses to hold all his wealth. He did this not knowing that very night he would die, and face God's judgment. It is far more important that we do what God wants us to do, to tell others about Him, so we can lay up treasure in heaven.

Answer the following questions

1. What is hypocrisy?

2. Who did Jesus say to fear?

3. Who will the Son of man confess before the angels of God?

4. What does a man's life not consist of?

5. What did the rich man say to his soul?

Day 113

Read Luke 12:22-40

Swordfighter's Tip:
When Jesus said to take no thought for tomorrow, He was saying we should not worry about how God will take care of us. If God will take care of all of the animals, then He will take care of us. We still need to work to supply our needs, but we need to trust God to supply the work.

Answer the following questions

1. What is more than meat?

2. What was Solomon not arrayed like?

3. What is the Father's good pleasure?

4. Where will your heart be?

5. When will the Son of man come?

Day 114

Read Luke 12:41-59

Swordfighter's Tip:
When Jesus said He was come to send division, He was saying that some people will not accept the truth. Jesus did not say that we should accept everything, but that we should stand firmly for the truth. The truth divides. The only way for Christians to get along with everyone is to abandon the truth. That does not mean Christians should be argumentative, but that we should stand for the truth when called to.

Answer the following questions

1. Which servant is blessed?

2. When will the lord of the servant come?

3. To whom is much required?

4. Who will be divided against the son?

5. Who will the judge deliver you to?

Day 115

Read Luke 13:1-17

Swordfighter's Tip:

The Pharisees were upset that Jesus healed a crippled woman on the Sabbath day. They were looking for any excuse to attack Jesus because He had called them out on their hypocrisy. People looked to the Pharisees as the best people around, but Jesus showed many of their problems. He again exposes their hypocrisy by saying that if they would rescue their livestock on the Sabbath day, than Jesus would heal someone who had been suffering for years.

Answer the following questions

1. How many died in Siloam?

2. What tree was planted in the vineyard?

3. How long had the woman had the spirit of infirmity?

4. Why did the ruler of the synagogue answer with indignation?

5. Who were ashamed?

Day 116

Read Luke 13:18-35

Swordfighter's Tip:

When Jesus spoke about what the kingdom of God would be like, He was speaking about the Church on earth. He compared it to a mustard seed, which is incredibly tiny. Yet that mustard seed when planted will grow into a great tree. He compared it to a bit of yeast, which will make a whole batch of bread rise. This is what a Christian should be. Though we may be tiny, when we let God work in us, His work affects all around us.

Answer the following questions

1. What happened to the mustard seed?

2. How much meal did the woman put the leaven into?

3. Where did Jesus journey to?

4. Who shall be first?

5. When would Jesus be perfected?

Day 117

Read Luke 14:1-14

Swordfighter's Tip:

Jesus warned His followers to stay humble. He gave an example of a wedding. At that time, weddings were huge feasts that lasted for several days. Many weddings would have more than one room for the party because they were so large. Jesus told his disciples to choose one of the less important rooms first. Christians should not think highly of themselves, nor put ourselves out as someone great.

Answer the following questions

1. When did Jesus go into the house?

2. What did Jesus ask the Pharisees?

3. Which room should the disciples not sit in?

4. Who shall be abased?

5. Who did Jesus say to call when making a feast?

Day 118

Read Luke 14:15-35

Swordfighter's Tip:
When Jesus said that if you don't hate your parents, you can't follow Him, He was not speaking literally. He was saying that our love and devotion for Him should be such that it seems that we hate our family. We need to put God first in everything. To often we want to put God in second place to sports, or games, or other types of fun. God needs to be our first priority.

Answer the following questions

1. Who made a great supper?

2. What did the second man invited to the supper say?

3. Who would not taste of the great man's supper?

4. What does a man do before building a tower?

5. Who cannot be Jesus' disciple?

Day 119

Read Luke 15:1-32

Swordfighter's Tip:

The Pharisees could not understand how Jesus would associate Himself with sinners. Publicans were tax collectors. They were seen as the lowest form of scum because they helped the Roman occupiers, and also regularly overcharged people on their taxes. Jesus used a set of stories to show that God rejoices in anyone who chooses to follow Him. No matter what a man may have done, God rejoices when a sinner gets saved.

Answer the following questions

1. Who drew near to Jesus?

2. How many sheep does the man leave in the wilderness?

3. How many sons did the man have?

4. What had the father killed?

5. Who was lost and found?

Day 120

Read Luke 16:1-31

Swordfighter's Tip:
When the rich man in hell begged Abraham to send someone back from the dead to tell his brothers to turn to God, Abraham responded they had the law and the prophets. This referred to the Bible as it existed then. God's truth is told us in the Bible. If people refuse to accept its teachings, they won't choose to follow God.

Answer the following questions

1. What was the steward accused of?

2. How much did the first debtor owe?

3. What can a servant not serve?

4. Who did the rich man see afar off?

5. How many brothers did the rich man have?

Day 121

Read Luke 17:1-19

Swordfighter's Tip:

When the disciples asked Jesus to increase their faith, Jesus taught them that it is not the amount of faith one has, but who he has the faith in. Jesus uses the example of a mustard seed. It is one of the tiniest of seeds, barely larger than a grain of sand. Jesus said that if you have that much faith in God, you can command great trees to be cast in the ocean. This is not literal, but an example of what God can do through those who have faith in Him.

Answer the following questions

1. What is impossible?

2. What did the apostles say to Jesus?

3. Where did Jesus pass through the midst of?

4. What did Jesus say to the lepers?

5. How many lepers turned back?

Day 122

Read Luke 17:20-37

Swordfighter's Tip:

The Pharisees demanded to know when the kingdom of God, or specifically when Christ will come to rule over all of the earth. Jesus answered them that it would come when no one was looking for it. Some people would beg for it to come, but most people will ignore God entirely. Christians will already have left the earth in the rapture, but there will be many people saved after this event.

Answer the following questions

1. What comes not with observation?

2. What did they do in the days of No'-e?

3. What happened the same day Lot went out of Soddom?

4. Who will lose his life?

5. Where will the eagles be gathered together?

Day 123

Read Luke 18:1-17

Swordfighter's Tip:
Jesus told the story of the unjust judge to show us how God reacts to our prayers. If an unjust judge was willing to grant a widow's request, so will God grant us ours. Sometimes God wants us to show our sincerity by asking often. Sometimes God waits because His time has not come.

Answer the following questions

1. What ought men to always do?

2. Who will God avenge?

3. Who went into the temple to pray?

4. What did the publican say?

5. Who shall be exalted?

Day 124

Read Luke 18:18-43

Swordfighter's Tip:

A rich ruler came to Jesus and asked Him what was needed to gain eternal life. Jesus listed a few of the commandments that God had given. When the rich ruler says he had done so, Jesus told him to sell all his belongings and give them to the poor. God does not hate the rich, nor does He demand that all of us give up all of our possessions. Jesus knew the ruler's heart. He knew the ruler put his wealth ahead of God. His wealth had become his idol. He had put his wealth ahead of God.

Answer the following questions

1. What did the ruler call Jesus?

2. What is easier than a rich man entering the kingdom of God?

3. What would be accomplished when Jesus went up to Jerusalem?

4. Where did they meet the blind beggar?

5. What did the blind man call Jesus?

Day 125

Read Luke 19:1-27

Swordfighter's Tip:

The disciples did not know why Jesus had come to earth the first time. They thought that when Jesus entered Jerusalem, He would throw out the Romans and rule the world as their Messiah, or deliverer. They didn't know that Jesus had come to earth to die for our sins. The next time Jesus comes to earth, He will rule the world as our King of kings.

Answer the following questions

1. Who was chief among the publicans?

2. Who is come to seek and to save?

3. How much money did the nobleman give his servants?

4. How much money did the second servant earn?

5. Who did the nobleman say to give the pound of the unfaithful servant?

Day 126

Read Luke 19:28-48

Swordfighter's Tip:

Jesus looked at Jerusalem and spoke about what would happen to the city. He said that her enemies would surround the city and tear it down because the people of the city would reject Him. God keeps His promises and what Jesus said would happen, occurred in A.D. 70. The Romans surrounded the city with a wall to keep anyone from escaping, and through the course of the battle tore down the temple completely.

Answer the following questions

1. What was the mount called?

2. What did the owner's say as the disciples were loosing the colt?

3. What did Jesus would say would cry out if the disciples were silent?

4. Who did Jesus cast out of the temple?

5. Who were attentive to hear Jesus?

Day 127

Read Luke 20:1-26

Swordfighter's Tip:

After Jesus turned away all of the attempts of the Pharisees to trap Jesus, they tried another tactic. They had some of their number dress like the rest of the crowd and ask Jesus if people should pay taxes. If Jesus said yes, then the crowd who hated the Romans would be upset. If Jesus said no, than the Romans would kill Jesus for preaching against them. Jesus answered in a way that pleased both groups.

Answer the following questions

1. Who came to Jesus?

2. What were the people persuaded about John?

3. How many servants did the Lord of the vineyard send?

4. What is become the head of the corner?

5. What should you render to Caesar?

Day 128

Read Luke 20:27-47

Swordfighter's Tip:

The Saducees were a group that denied the truth of the Bible. They believed that death was the end, and wanted to show the possibility of life after death was absurd. Jesus answered them by showing they did not understand the Bible, because they had not considered any reading that did not meet their predecided beliefs.

Answer the following questions

1. What do the Saducees deny?

2. Who died last?

3. What is God the God of?

4. Who did David call Lord?

5. What do the scribes love?

Day 129

Read Luke 21:1-15

Swordfighter's Tip:

Jesus drew attention to the woman putting two mites into the offering box. Several rich people had gone before her, putting large amounts of money in the box. Jesus chose to praise the woman who put just a small amount of money into the offering, because she gave all she had. God looks to what people do with what they have, and praises faithfulness.

Answer the following questions

1. How much did the widow cast into the treasury?

2. What was the temple adorned with?

3. What will rise against nation?

4. What would the disciples be brought before?

5. What would the disciples' adversaries not be able to resist?

Fun Fact: A mite would be about $1.50 today

Day 130

Read Luke 21:16-38

Swordfighter's Tip:

Jesus warned the disciples what would happen before He returned. Before Jesus comes to reign on earth, there will be a time of great trials. Many people will die in this time. Eventually the world will gather around Israel to fight against her. That is when Jesus will return to earth to reign on earth.

Answer the following questions

1. Who would the disciples be betrayed by?

2. When will you know desolation draws nigh?

3. Where will there be signs?

4. When do you know summer is at hand?

5. Where did Jesus abide at night?

Day 131

Read Luke 22:1-23

Swordfighter's Tip:

Jews from all around the world had gathered at Jerusalem to celebrate the feast of Passover. This feast reminded them of when God delivered Israel from slavery in Egypt. Jesus used this feast to give us something to remember. We eat the bread to remember the injuries Jesus suffered when He was crucified. We drink the juice to remember the blood Jesus shed for our sins.

Answer the following questions

1. Who did the chief priests fear?

2. What did Judas Iscariot seek opportunity for?

3. What would the man be bearing?

4. Who sat down with Jesus?

5. What did the disciples enquire amongst themselves?

Day 132

Read Luke 22:24-46

Swordfighter's Tip:

In the garden of Gethsemene, the Jesus showed His humanity. Jesus was completely human, but also completely God. As a human, Jesus knew all the pain and suffering He would face. He asked His Father to if possible let Him not have to face it all. He then submitted Himself to His Father's will.

Answer the following questions

1. What strife rose among the disciples?

2. Who did Satan desire to sift?

3. How many swords did the disciples have?

4. What strengthened Jesus?

5. How did Jesus find the disciples?

Day 133

Read Luke 22:47-71

Swordfighter's Tip:

Peter had a great love for Jesus. When Jesus was arrested, Peter followed the guards who arrested Him. While he was watching the trial, people around recognized him as one of Jesus' followers. Peter, out of fear denied that he knew Jesus. He did so very strongly. Peter was just a man, who did great things for Jesus, because Jesus accepted him, and used him despite his faults. Jesus will use any of us who love Him as well.

Answer the following questions

1. Who drew near to Jesus to kiss Him?

2. Who did one of the disciples smite?

3. Who beheld Peter by the fire first?

4. What happened when Peter denied Jesus the third time?

5. Where did the chief priests take Jesus?

Day 134

Read Luke 23:1-26

Swordfighter's Tip:
Pilate did not want to deal with Jesus. He could not find a single law Jesus had broken. He tried to pass Jesus off to Herod, because Jesus was from Herod's region. Herod sent Jesus back to Pilate. Some years before, Pilate had stripped the Jews of the authority to execute someone on their own. Now, his political leader had fallen out of favor, and Pilate had to fear the Jews. Thus, he took every effort to release Jesus, but eventually had to have Him crucified.

Answer the following questions

1. What did Pilate ask Jesus?

2. Where was Herod?

3. What did Herod array Jesus in?

4. What was Barabbas in prison for?

5. Who did they lay hold of to bear the cross after Jesus?

Day 135

Read Luke 23:27-56

Swordfighter's Tip:
Two men were crucified with Jesus. They show our reactions to Jesus. One man railed against Jesus, and said he would believe in Jesus, if He would save him from the cross. The other recognized Jesus as God Himself, and asked for salvation. We have the same choice. We can believe in Jesus, or reject Him. What will your choice be?

Answer the following questions

1. Who followed Jesus?

2. Where did they take Jesus?

3. What did the superscription say?

4. What did the centurion say?

5. Where did the women come from?

Day 136

Read Luke 24:1-32

Swordfighter's Tip:

After Jesus rose from the dead, he visited two men traveling to Emmaus. They were trying to understand all that had happened in Jerusalem that week. God kept them from recognizing Jesus while He showed them everything that happened was promised. Throughout the Old Testament, God told what would happen to Jesus. Beginning in Genesis, God promised someone who would be the sacrifice for our sins.

Answer the following questions

1. What day of the week did they go to the Sepulchre?

2. What question did the two men in shining garments ask?

3. How far was Emmaus from Jerusalem?

4. Where did Jesus expound to the two men from?

5. What happened when the two men's eyes were opened?

 *Fun Fact: A furlong is about 600 feet.*

Day 137

Read Luke 24:33-53

Swordfighter's Tip:
After Jesus rose from the dead, He appeared to His disciples. He had them touch the wounds on His body, and He even ate a small meal with them. He did this to show them He was no ghost, but had truly risen from the dead. Some men would claim that Jesus was only a spirit, but by eating with multiple people, Jesus proved He was truly alive. A ghost can't eat food. We do not serve a ghost, or a dead God, but we serve a risen Lord.

Answer the following questions

1. Where did they return to?

2. Who stood in the midst of them?

3. What did they give Jesus to eat?

4. How long were the disciples to tarry in Jerusalem?

5. Where did Jesus lead them to?

Introduction to John

The Gospel of John was written by the Apostle John. He was one of the original twelve disciples, a good friend of Peter and Andrew, along with his brother James. He and his brother James were named "The sons of thunder" by Jesus because they were so passionate in their devotion to Him. John was the last of the twelve Apostles to die, having been exiled to an island to try and stop him from preaching.

The Gospel of John has many differences from the Synoptic, or similar, Gospels. It was probably the last Gospel written, but its date is really unknown. The Gospel of John is written to emphasize that Jesus was God Himself, come to earth in human form. John writes about more times that Jesus claimed to be God than the other writers. John emphasizes the power of God, how no man could kill Jesus, but rather that He willingly gave His life as the perfect sacrifice for our sins.

Day 138

Read John 1:1-34

Swordfighter's Tip:
Who was John the Baptist? John was the second cousin of Jesus. He was sent to earth for a special reason. The Old Testament had prophecsed multiple times that before Jesus came, someone would come before Him. John was that person. He preached to everyone that Jesus would be coming soon, and they needed to get their lives right. He baptized, or dunked people in water as a sign they were changing their lives. We need to warn people that Jesus has come, and will come again.

Answer the following questions

1. Who was with God in the beginning?

2. What was the name of the man sent from God as a witness?

3. Who was made flesh and dwelt among us?

4. What did John baptize with?

5. Who did John say was the Lamb of God?

Day 139

Read John 1:35-51

Swordfighter's Tip:
Who was Nathaniel? We know very little about him. Jesus praised him for being a man without guile, or being extremely honest. It is believed by many that he was called Bartholomew in the other Gospels. He was the first to declare Jesus to be God. Like almost all the apostles, he was killed for preaching about Jesus.

Answer the following questions

1. What did Jesus say to the two disciples who followed Him?

2. Who was one of the two who heard John speak?

3. Where was Phillip from?

4. What did Phillip tell Nathaniel?

5. What did Nathaniel call Jesus?

Day 140

Read John 2:1-25

Swordfighter's Tip:

This is the first time Jesus chased people out of the temple. All Jewish men were required to pay a tax to help with upkeep of the Temple. By Jesus' time, they were required to use a specific coin to pay this tax. A group of people at the Temple would change your money to this special coin for a fee. God does not want people to get rich by making special rules to worship God.

Answer the following questions

1. Where was the marriage at?

2. How many water pots were there?

3. Where did Jesus go after He left the marriage?

4. For what feast did Jesus go to Jerusalem?

5. How long did it take to build the temple?

Day 141

Read John 3:1-36

Swordfighter's Tip:

Who was Nicodemus? He is spoken of three times in John. He was a Pharisee, a group that started out trying to follow God as the world around them rejected Him. He was also in the Sanhedrin, which was the ruling council of the Jews. He came to Jesus seeking to understand His teachings. At first he came by night, so no could see him. Later, he reminded the other Pharisees to follow the law before condemning Jesus. The last time we see him, he was helping bury Jesus.

Answer the following questions

1. What did Nicodemus call Jesus?

2. What must a man be born of to enter the kingdom of God?

3. What did Moses lift up in the wilderness?

4. What does every one that does evil hate?

5. What does he whom God sent speak?

Did you know? "Rabbi" means teacher.

Day 142

Read John 4:1-30

Swordfighter's Tip:

When Jesus said He needed to go through Samaria, people around Him would have been amazed. Jews did not like Samaritans, they hated them. Samaritans were only partially Jewish, having intermarried with Gentiles. When Jews needed to travel to that area, they would go out of their way to travel around Samaria. If they absolutely had to travel through there, They would never talk to a Samaritan. Jesus cares for everyone, not our prejudices.

Answer the following questions

1. Where did Jesus leave?

2. What was the name of the well Jesus stopped by?

3. How many husbands had the woman had?

4. How must people worship God?

5. What did the woman leave when she went into the city?

Day 143

Read John 4:31-54

Swordfighter's Tip:
Jesus saw a need to preach to others. It satisfied Him to tell others about Him. He tried to get it across to the disciples the need for urgency. We can't just put off telling others about Jesus, we need to tell them now.

Answer the following questions

1. What is Jesus' meat?

2. What did the woman testify to the Samaritans?

3. Where does a prophet have no honour?

4. Where was the nobleman's son at?

5. At what hour was the son healed?

Day 144

Read John 5:1-16

Swordfighter's Tip:

There was a crippled man who desired to be healed. He stayed by a pool that an angel would regularly stop by and heal the first person to get in the water. Jesus saw him, and healed him. As he was carrying his cot to his home people stopped him, because work was forbidden on the Sabbath day. The Jewish leaders had created many rules as to what work was. They wanted to kill Jesus because He didn't follow their rules. He followed God's law, not man's rules added to it.

Answer the following questions

1. What was the name of the pool?

2. How long had the man had the infirmity?

3. When was the man made whole?

4. What did the Jews tell the man was not lawful?

5. Why did the Jews seek to kill Jesus?

Day 145

Read John 5:17-47

Swordfighter's Tip:
One of the biggest problems the Jews had with Jesus was that He claimed to be God. They could partially accept a prophet who did miracles, but they refused to see that Jesus was God. C.S. Lewis gave the proposition that Jesus was either a liar, a lunatic, or Lord, because He claimed to be God so often. The Jews decided Jesus had to be a liar, but Jesus proved He was Lord. Jesus was God come to earth to die for out sins.

Answer the following questions

1. Who can do nothing of himself?

2. Who honoureth not the Father?

3. What did John bear witness to?

4. What was the greater witness than John?

5. The Jews would believe Jesus, if they had believed whom?

Day 146

Read John 6:1-21

Swordfighter's Tip:
Jesus and His disciples traveled into the wilderness the people followed Him. They wanted to hear His teachings, and see the miracles He did. Jesus saw them and realized the day was growing late. He wanted to test His disciples when He asked them how they would feed the mass of people there. One of the disciples said it would take a huge amount of money just to buy food to feed them. They forgot the power of God to provide.

Answer the following questions

1. What is the sea of Galilee also known as?

2. Which feast was nigh?

3. Who was Simon Peter's brother?

4. How many baskets did they fill with fragments of the loaves?

5. Where did the disciples sail towards?

 *Fun Fact: 200 pennyworth would be about 24,000 dollars.*

Day 147

Read John 6:22-40

Swordfighter's Tip:
The people did not get the point of Jesus feeding the multitude. They claimed that Moses provided for the people in the wilderness, forgetting that it was God that provided the manna. Jesus than explained that just as God provided bread to feed Israel, so He sent Jesus to provide eternal life to people who believe in Him.

Answer the following questions

1. How many boats were on the other side of the sea?

2. Where did the other boats come from?

3. What is the work of God?

4. What did the Jews fathers eat in the desert?

5. What is the will of He who sent Jesus?

Day 148

Read John 6:41-71

Swordfighter's Tip:
When Jesus said that unless you eat His flesh, and drink His blood, many people walked away from Him. They wanted a victorious leader who would overthrow the Romans. They did see that Jesus was not speaking literally, but was telling what He would say at the Last Supper. The only way to have eternal life is to believe in the suffering and resurrection of Jesus.

Answer the following questions

1. Why did the Jews murmur against Jesus?

2. Who is the bread of life?

3. What did the Jew's fathers eat in the wilderness?

4. Where in Capernaum did Jesus teach these things?

5. Who did Jesus say was a devil?

Day 149

Read John 7:1-31

Swordfighter's Tip:

When people tried to capture or kill Jesus in His early ministry, they were not able to. Sometimes, Jesus just walked right through them. He said, His time had not come. When Jesus went to the cross, it was purely by His will. No man took Jesus' life, He willingly gave it up.

Answer the following questions

1. What feast was at hand?

2. Did Jesus' brothers believe in Him?

3. Why does the world hate Jesus?

4. Why did no one speak openly of Jesus?

5. What are we not to judge according to?

Day 150

Read John 7:32-53

Swordfighter's Tip:

When Jesus was teaching, He began to foretell what would happen to Him. People could not yet see it because they were looking for a victorious conqueror to deliver them. They also did not know one detail. When some people wondered if He was the promised Christ, or deliverer, they knew He had grown up in Galilee, and that the Christ was prophesied to be born in Bethlehem. They did not realize that Jesus had been born in Bethlehem, due to Caesar Augustus' census.

Answer the following questions

1. Who sent officers to take Jesus?

2. What was not yet given?

3. Who laid hands on Jesus?

4. Who are cursed?

5. What did Nicodemus say?

Day 151

Read John 8:1-32

Swordfighter's Tip:
When the Pharisees questioned Jesus, He pointed out that they couldn't understand Him, because they did not know the Father. The Pharisees outwardly worshiped God. They were known to follow every piece of their traditions. But, they didn't know God. They had let outward actions blind them to a relationship with God. Jesus made it clear that only by truly desiring to follow God, can one know Him. To have a relationship with God should be our greatest desire.

Answer the following questions

1. Where did Jesus go early in the morning?

2. Who did Jesus say should cast the first stone?

3. Where did Jesus say those who follow Him would not walk?

4. Why did no one lay hands on Jesus?

5. What shall make you free?

Day 152

Read John 8:33-59

Swordfighter's Tip:
When Jesus said, "Before Abraham was, I am," the Jews present tried to attack Him. They did this because Jesus had just openly claimed to be God Himself. When Moses asked God for His name, when he went to demand Israel's release from Pharaoh, God told him to say I Am had sent him. God was known in the Old Testament as I Am. Every Jew knew this. They were not willing to believe Jesus was God, so they wanted to kill Him.

Answer the following questions

1. Who is the servant of sin?

2. What did the Jews say they were not born of?

3. Who did Jesus say the Pharisees father was?

4. What will happen to a man who keeps Jesus' sayings?

5. What did Jesus do when the Jews took up stones to throw at Him?

Day 153

Read John 9:1-17

Swordfighter's Tip:
When Jesus lived, most people believed that if a person had any handicap, then someone must have sinned. If a person became handicapped after birth, he must have committed some sin for God to judge him. If he was born with a handicap, either he or his parents must have sinned. Some handicaps do come from sin, but as Jesus said, some come because God wants to be glorified, either through that persons struggles, or through healing it.

Answer the following questions

1. Who is the light of the world?

2. What did Jesus anoint the eyes of the person with?

3. Where did Jesus tell the man to go?

4. Who did they bring the man to?

5. What day of the week did Jesus heal the man?

Day 154

Read John 9:18-41

Swordfighter's Tip:

 *The Old Testament Law commanded that the Sabbath day, or Saturday be kept holy to God. People were not allowed to do any work, but they were to rest and remember that God freed them from slavery. Over the years, the Pharisees had added many rules as to what was work. They were upset that Jesus had healed the blind man on the Sabbath day. They could not see that God did not see saving someone as work.*

Answer the following questions

1. What did the Jews not believe until they called the man's parents?

2. What had the Jews agreed?

3. Who did the Pharisees say they were the disciples of?

4. Who does God not hear?

5. Why did Jesus say the Pharisees sin remains?

Day 155

Read John 10:1-21

Swordfighter's Tip:

When they heard Jesus speak, many of the Jewish people were divided. Some people saw Jesus as a prophet, like God had sent before. Yet no prophet had claimed the authority Jesus did. Some people saw Him as the promised deliverer, but Jesus spoke of dying, and did not act like He would overthrow the Roman conquerors. Some who heard Him thought He must be possessed by demons because He was so strange. Others saw that demons could not do what Jesus did.

Answer the following questions

1. How does the robber enter the sheepfold?

2. Whose voice do the sheep know?

3. Who is the door of the sheep?

4. Why does the hireling flee?

5. Why does the Father love Jesus?

Day 156

Read John 10:22:42

Swordfighter's Tip:

Throughout the Gospel, John highlights Jesus claiming to be God. Here again some of the Jewish leaders wanted to kill Jesus because He claimed to be God. Jesus pointed to all the evidence of His miracles to show that what He said was true. Though many men may try to deny it, Jesus was not just a good man, or a teacher, He was God come on earth in human form.

Answer the following questions

1. What feast was Jesus at?

2. What bears witness of Jesus?

3. Who is greater than all?

4. What cannot be broken?

5. Where did John first baptize?

Day 157

Read John 11:1-27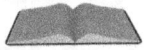

Swordfighter's Tip:
There was a Jewish tradition that the soul of a person stayed near the body for three days. When Jesus heard that Lazarus was sick, He waited for several days before beginning to travel to Lazarus. Jesus got there four days after Lazarus had died. Jesus did these things to show the true power of God. No matter bad our problems may seem, God will come through in His time.

Answer the following questions

1. Where was Lazarus from?

2. How long did Jesus wait when He heard Lazarus was sick?

3. Why does a man who walks in the day not stumble?

4. What did Thomas say when Jesus said they would go see Lazarus?

5. Who is the resurrection?

Day 158

Read John 11:28-57

Swordfighter's Tip:

When Jesus raised Lazarus from the dead, even more people began to take notice of Him. Some of the Jewish leaders were scared that the Romans would remove them from power if to many people followed Jesus. They joined with those who did not believe in Jesus in desiring to kill Jesus. At this time, Jesus left traveling in public for a little while, because He knew when He had to die.

Answer the following questions

1. What did Mary tell Jesus?

2. What lay upon the grave?

3. What was bound on Lazarus' face?

4. Who was the high priest?

5. What commandment had both the high priest and the Pharisees given?

Day 159

Read John 12:1-19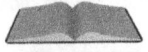

Swordfighter's Tip:

The Jewish religious leaders had completely abandoned following God. They were upset that Jesus preached against their hypocrisy. They saw how the people followed Him, and saw the miracles. It came to a head when they plotted to kill Lazarus. The figured that if he was dead, the people wouldn't be reminded that Jesus had raised him from the dead.

Answer the following questions

1. How many days before the passover did Jesus enter Bethany?

2. How much did Judas say the ointment should be sold for?

3. Who would the disciples not always have with them?

4. How does the daughter of Sion's King come?

5. Who did the Pharisees say had gone after Jesus?

Day 160

Read John 12:20-50

Swordfighter's Tip:

The Jewish people had just cheered for Jesus as He entered the city. They heard Him saying that He would be killed. They had always been taught that the Christ, or deliverer would come to chase out all of the invaders who had ruled them for the last long while. They had not read the many passages in the Old Testament that show the Messiah would die for all men. Jesus had come to earth to die for all men's sins, by being the perfect sacrifice.

Answer the following questions

1. What hour did Jesus say had come?

2. What did the voice from heaven say?

3. What had the people heard out of the law?

4. What did the chief rulers love more than the praise of God?

5. What will judge the person who rejects Jesus in the last day?

Day 161

Read John 13:1-38

Swordfighter's Tip:
When Jesus lived, people had to walk nearly everywhere. When you visited someone, they would provide a servant to wash your feet from all of the dirt of walking everywhere. This job was usually handed to the lowest servant, because it was such a dirty job. When Jesus chose to do this for the disciples, He was setting the example that His leaders are to lead by service. No Christian should refuse to do something for God because it is beneath them.

Answer the following questions

1. What did Jesus gird Himself with?

2. What more than his feet did Simon Peter ask Jesus to wash?

3. Who is not greater than his lord?

4. Who did Jesus give the sop to?

5. What new commandment had Jesus given His disciples?

Day 162

Read John 14:1-31

Swordfighter's Tip:
Jesus here promised the coming of the Holy Spirit when He said the Father will send the Comforter. At this time, the Holy Spirit did not live in believers. They disciples still had Jesus with them for a little while. Jesus promised that after He left, the Holy Spirit would dwell in believers. At the day of Pentecost this happened. Today we have the Holy Spirit living in us.

Answer the following questions

1. What are in Jesus' Father's house?

2. Who is the truth?

3. What will the person who believes do?

4. What did the other Judas (not Iscariot) ask Jesus?

5. Who is the Comforter?

Day 163

Read John 15:1-27

Swordfighter's Tip:

Jesus named the disciples, friends. A friend is far more than a servant. A servant does what he is told because he has to. A friend wants to help his friend. Jesus wants us to be more than servants, doing what we He commanded because we have to. He wants us to be friends, doing what He asks, because we love Him. He set the example of love, by giving all He could when He died for us.

Answer the following questions

1. Who is the true vine?

2. What happens to the man who does not abide in Jesus?

3. What greater love can no man have?

4. Who did the world hate before the disciples?

5. With what cause did the Jews hate Jesus?

Day 164

Read John 16:1-33

Swordfighter's Tip:

One role of the Holy Spirit is to guide all men towards what is true. When you ask Him to and allow Him to, God through the Holy Spirit will help show you what He wants for your lives. One important thing to remember: God will never contradict Himself. What the Holy Spirit reveals will not disagree with what the Bible says anywhere.

Answer the following questions

1. Where would the put the disciples out of?

2. What would the Comforter reprove the world of?

3. Who will glorify Jesus?

4. What would be turned into joy?

5. Who has overcome the world?

Day 165

Read John 17:1-26

Swordfighter's Tip:

When Jesus prayed His last prayer for the disciples, He knew that they would be hated. Jesus was hated by many because He dared to challenge the rituals that people had created. Jesus wants all men to truly love God, not just go through motions. Jesus did not ask God to spare the disciples from problems, He only promised to stand by them when people hated them. God does not want us to live separate from people, but to live among them, showing God's love to them.

Answer the following questions

1. What has the Father given the Son power over?

2. What did Jesus have with the Father before the world began?

3. What did Jesus pray the Holy Father would keep?

4. What is the Father's word?

5. What has Jesus declared?

Day 166

Read John 18:1-18

Swordfighter's Tip:
When the guards came to arrest Jesus, Jesus asked them who they were looking for. Jesus them told them "I am he." Jesus then revealed His full power the guards. The guards fell down at the sight of God's power. Jesus then willingly went with the guards. No person on earth could force Jesus to go with them. When they tried to kill Him before, Jesus walked right through them. Jesus willingly went, because He knew He had to die for our sins.

Answer the following questions

1. What brook did Jesus cross over?

2. From whom did Judas receive the band of men?

3. What was the servant's name?

4. Who did they lead Jesus to first?

5. What had the servants made a fire from?

Day 167

Read John 18:19-40

Swordfighter's Tip:
"I find no fault in Him." No truer words were spoken. When the Jewish leaders brought Jesus to be executed, Pilate could find no law Jesus had broken. The only crime the Jewish leaders could convict Jesus of was telling the truth, when He claimed to be God. Jesus broke no laws, nor did He commit any sin in His 33 years on earth. This is how Jesus could pay for our sins. Because Jesus had no sin, He could be the perfect sacrifice for out sins.

Answer the following questions

1. What did the high priest ask Jesus about?

2. Where had Annas sent Jesus?

3. What hall did they take Jesus to?

4. What is Jesus' kingdom not of?

5. What was Barabbas' crime?

Day 168

Read John 19:1-22

Swordfighter's Tip:
Pilate understood some of who Jesus was. He saw that Jesus was special. He indicated this when he put the sign up on Jesus' cross. It was common to put a sign up indicating what the person being crucified was guilty of. The Jewish leaders did not want the sign to indicate that Jesus was the King of the Jews, because they rejected Him. But Pilate, guided by God, put the truth up. Jesus was the King of the Jews, and one day He will return to rule the whole world.

Answer the following questions

1. What did the soldiers smite Jesus with?

2. What law did the Jews say Jesus had broken

3. What hour was it when Pilate said, "Behold your King?"

4. What is the place of the skull called in Hebrew?

5. What did Pilate say when the Jews complained about the title he wrote?

Day 169

Read John 19:23-42

Swordfighter's Tip:

When Jesus died on the cross, His last words were, "It is finished." Jesus then gave up the ghost. No one took Jesus' life, He gave it away. When He said it was finished, He was saying the commandment was fulfilled, the debt was payed. There was nothing man could do to pay this debt. No man could be this sacrifice, because only a perfect man without sin could die for the sins of the world. Jesus lived with out sin and when He died, He proclaimed the debt was paid.

Answer the following questions

1. How many parts did the soldiers divide Jesus garments into?

2. How many women stood by the cross?

3. What did Jesus say when He drank the vinegar?

4. Who asked Pilate for Jesus' body?

5. What was in the garden?

Day 170

Read John 20:1-31

Swordfighter's Tip:

Jesus was buried right before the Sabbath day began, and there was not enough time to properly prepare the body. At that time, when someone was buried, they were wrapped in cloth with fragrant herbs to help with the smell, and they were laid on a shelf in a cave carved out of rock. A large stone was then put over the entrance to seal the grave. Two ladies went on Sunday morning to finish the work on Jesus' body, where they found the tombstone moved and the body gone.

Answer the following questions

1. What day of the week did Mary Magdalene come to the tomb?

2. Who did not stop at the door of the tomb?

3. What did Jesus ask Mary?

4. Who was not with the disciples when Jesus first appeared?

5. Why were these things written?

Day 171

Read John 21:1-25

Swordfighter's Tip:

After Jesus rose from the dead, He appeared briefly to the disciples. He then disappeared. While waiting for Jesus to return and tell them what to do, Peter announced he was going fishing. This was not a hobby like it is today for many people, but his job. Peter announced he was going back to his job as a fisherman. Many of the disciples had been fishermen, and they joined him. When Jesus appeared a second time, Peter jumped from the boat to go back to Jesus.

Answer the following questions

1. Where did Jesus show himself to the disciples again?

2. What did Peter put on when he heard it was the Lord speaking to them?

3. How many fish were in the net?

4. How many times did Jesus ask Peter, "Lovest thou me?"

5. What could the word not contain the books written about?

www.ingramcontent.com/pod-product-compliance
Lightning Source LLC
Chambersburg PA
CBHW081154290426
44108CB00018B/2547